DATE DUE

Dictators

Other Books in the History Makers Series:

Dictators.

By Robert Green

Lucent Books
P.O. Box 289011, San Diego, CA 92198-9011

Library of Congress Cataloging-in-Publication Data

Green, Robert, 1969–
    Dictators / Robert Green.
        p.   cm. — (History makers)
    Includes bibliographical references (p.) and index.
    Summary: Discusses six dictators of the modern world, including
Francisco Franco, Adolf Hitler, Joseph Stalin, Mao Zedong, Fidel Castro,
and Saddam Hussein, and examines the effects of their actions on their
countries.
    ISBN 1-56006-594-X (lib bdg.)
    1. Dictators—Biography—Juvenile literature.] 2. Twentieth-century
Biography—Juvenile literature. [1. Dictators.] I. Title. II. Series.
    D412.6.G69   2000
    920'.009'04—dc21
                                                                    99-38361
                                                                    CIP

Printed in the U.S.A.

Cover photo: Center: Saddam Hussein, clockwise from top: Mao Zedong,
Adolf Hitler, Francisco Franco, Joseph Stalin

CONTENTS

FOREWORD

The literary form most often referred to as "multiple biography" was perfected in the first century A.D. by Plutarch, a perceptive and talented moralist and historian who hailed from the small town of Chaeronea in central Greece. His most famous work, *Parallel Lives*, consists of a long series of biographies of noteworthy ancient Greek and Roman statesmen and military leaders. Frequently, Plutarch compares a famous Greek to a famous Roman, pointing out similarities in personality and achievements. These expertly constructed and very readable tracts provided later historians and others, including playwrights like Shakespeare, with priceless information about prominent ancient personages and also inspired new generations of writers to tackle the multiple biography genre.

The Lucent History Makers series proudly carries on the venerable tradition handed down from Plutarch. Each volume in the series consists of a set of five to eight biographies of important and influential historical figures who were linked together by a common factor. In *Rulers of Ancient Rome*, for example, all the figures were generals, consuls, or emperors of either the Roman Republic or Empire; while the subjects of *Fighters Against American Slavery*, though they lived in different places and times, all shared the same goal, namely the eradication of human servitude. Mindful that politicians and military leaders are not (and never have been) the only people who shape the course of history, the editors of the series have also included representatives from a wide range of endeavors, including scientists, artists, writers, philosophers, religious leaders, and sports figures.

Each book is intended to give a range of figures—some well known, others less known; some who made a great impact on history, others who made only a small impact. For instance, by making Columbus's initial voyage possible, Spain's Queen Isabella I, featured in *Women Leaders of Nations*, helped to open up the New World to exploration and exploitation by the European powers. Unarguably, therefore, she made a major contribution to a series of events that had momentous consequences for the entire world. By contrast, Catherine II, the eighteenth-century Russian queen, and Golda Meir, the modern Israeli prime minister, did not play roles of global impact; however, their policies and actions significantly influenced the historical development of both their own countries and their regional neighbors. Regardless of their relative importance in the greater historical scheme, all of the figures chronicled in the History Makers series made contributions to posterity; and their public achievements, as well as what is known about their private lives, are presented and evaluated in light of the most recent scholarship.

In addition, each volume in the series is documented and substantiated by a wide array of primary and secondary source quotations. The primary source quotes enliven the text by presenting eyewitness views of the times and culture in which each history maker lived; while the secondary source quotes, taken from the works of respected modern scholars, offer expert elaboration and/or critical commentary. Each quote is footnoted, demonstrating to the reader exactly where biographers find their information. The footnotes also provide the reader with the means of conducting additional research. Finally, to further guide and illuminate readers, each volume in the series features photographs, two bibliographies, and a comprehensive index.

The History Makers series provides both students engaged in research and more casual readers with informative, enlightening, and entertaining overviews of individuals from a variety of circumstances, professions, and backgrounds. No doubt all of them, whether loved or hated, benevolent or cruel, constructive or destructive, will remain endlessly fascinating to each new generation seeking to identify the forces that shaped their world.

Six Ambitious Men

The six dictators covered in this book created societies with some remarkable similarities. To a man, they sacrificed their people's political and personal freedoms for what they decreed was the greater good of the nation. In all six countries under dictatorial rule—Spain, Germany, the Union of Soviet Socialist Republics, China, Cuba, and Iraq—the dictator directed the lives of his people and even controlled their ability to leave. Many dictators closed their borders altogether, making their countries prisons for their own citizens.

All six dictators relied on their armed forces to insulate them from foreign enemies and from their own people. In addition to the army, political police forces secretly watched their own countrymen, looking for the slightest deviation from the rigid life established for them by the dictator. Violence and the threat of violence ensured compliance, and fear became a hallmark of life under a dictator.

But the similarities of daily life in these dictatorships belies the unique ambitions of the six dictators. Each dictator has played a different role in modern history, and all six met with different degrees of success.

Francisco Franco, the most successful of all the Fascist leaders, staved off threats to the Catholic Church, the royal family, and the military in Spanish society for thirty-seven years. When social revolution threatened these institutions in Spain, he acted swiftly. And his successful rebellion installed him as the guardian of Spain's ancient institutions for the rest of his life. Franco saw himself as a benevolent dictator, and indeed his regime was less violent and less revolutionary than many other dictatorships. Through his reactionary government, Franco set out to preserve the old order—not to create a new society—and while he lived he largely succeeded.

Franco's moderation as a dictator stands in marked contrast to the madness of one of his contemporaries, Adolf Hitler. Hitler was a man consumed by hatred. With spellbinding oratory and an almost hypnotic power over the German people, he led his nation into an orgy of death and destruction. Brutality, racism, and even mass murder had occurred before, but his systematic genocide in mechanized factories of death marked a new low point for humanity. Ironically, Hitler was unusually successful at winning the support of his own people. With sheer force of will, he drew an entire nation into his evil dream and marched them into ruin. The Germans paid dearly for supporting Hitler. During Hitler's rule, 6.5 million Germans died as either a direct or indirect result of his insane policies. The Allied powers suffered more than double that number in their efforts to destroy Nazi Germany.

The equally brutal Joseph Stalin transformed the Soviet Union, the world's largest country, into an industrial power, but along the way he managed to kill more of his own countrymen than were killed by foreign invaders during World War II. Stalin's power was absolute, and his suspicious nature led him to use it brutally. He forced thousands, perhaps millions, of people to "confess" to imaginary crimes against the state and then executed them. Stalin also terrorized the rest of the world. Using an enormous military machine, he constantly threatened a third world war.

Stalin found a competitor for the lead role in world Communism in Mao Zedong. Mao transformed the world's most populous nation, China, into a Communist dictatorship. He temporarily restored

Francisco Franco (center) and Adolf Hitler (right) provide contrasting examples of Fascist dictatorships. Franco's rule was moderate and less violent than Hitler's extreme, hate-driven government.

SS troops parade before Heinrich Himmler and Adolf Hitler. Hitler's charisma won him the overwhelming support of his fellow Germans.

to China its ancient isolation from the rest of the world. And with China's borders shut, Mao entered into the world's largest experiment in social revolution, through which he attempted to change the path set by five thousand years of Chinese cultural history.

Fidel Castro carried the dream of world Communism into the Western Hemisphere. In the process, Castro became a mortal enemy of the United States by creating a Communist dictatorship just ninety miles off the coast of Florida. U.S. hostility toward Castro propelled him into a role on the international stage out of all proportion to the size of his nation.

Saddam Hussein has also managed to draw the wrath of the United States by trying to create a store of weapons of mass destruction in the volatile political atmosphere of the Middle East. Hussein is a strongman of the type that has reigned in one country or another for thousands of years. But he has staked out a place in the history of dictators because of his willingness to use the most gruesome biological and chemical weapons on his own people and because of his willingness to unleash naked aggression on his neighbors.

CHAPTER 1

The Dictator in the Twentieth Century

The twentieth century, which opened with such optimism and such great belief in the benevolent powers of technology, has seen the rise of some of the most sinister dictators and most destructive wars in the history of civilization. Totalitarian governments as well as democracies answered calls to war, sometimes with astonishing enthusiasm.

The elected leaders of democracies like Great Britain, France, and the United States believed that the rule of law should govern in the place of an absolute leader. However, this ideal of spreading representative government was abandoned frequently even by democratically elected leaders. In the interest of trade, the world's democracies often supported strongmen whose nations could provide stable markets for manufactured goods. And their hopes for spreading their form of government were also thwarted by dictators who concentrated power in their own hands.

Progress, so trumpeted at the outset of the century, seemed at times to do little more than provide new, more deadly weapons for the slaughter of man. Technological advances led to a general feeling of optimism among many people around the world at the start of the new century. But many of these advances in technology were put to use in wars in which dictatorships and democracies bled each other dry.

Dictators are hardly an aberration in the course of history. Throughout most of history, nations have been ruled by unelected officials. Kings, pharaohs, shahs, and emperors presided over their subjects with little regard for personal freedoms. Separated from their people by walls of ritual and by fortified palaces, these rulers were often deaf to their people's aspirations. Absolute power has proven just as seductive to twentieth-century dictators, who ruled with the backing of the military and gambled with their people's lives to advance their personal agendas.

A British biplane in combat during World War I. The devastating war wreaked havoc on the nations involved.

The catastrophic wars that marked the twentieth century with bloodshed on an unprecedented scale resulted largely from the ambition of leaders gambling through military means for greater land, wealth, and influence in world politics. World War I (1914–1918), for example, was the result of a clash of competing imperial powers that butchered each other over foreign colonies that they exploited for commercial gain.

Wars of Imperialism

At the outset of the century, imperialism was promoted by some of the very same countries that promoted the rule of law and the democratic election of government leaders. Great Britain, for example, ruled an empire around the globe through the use of its navy, even as its leaders were democratically elected at home. Though the British were fond of preaching the benefits of free-market trading and elected governments, they were willing to advance that agenda with devastating force. When foreign markets closed their ports to British trade goods, the British reopened them with city-leveling barrages from gunboats. When nations colonized by the British sought independence, Britain willingly used its army to suppress such movements.

The military advantages of the Western imperial powers over the countries of Asia, Africa, and the Americas resulted from the harnessing of natural resources toward the manufacture of labor-saving machines. The inventions and improvements of the twentieth century, like the airplane and the modern assembly line, were indeed marvelous. But military applications of new technologies followed close on the heels of the inventions themselves. A new branch of the military service, the air force, was created when airplanes flew reconnaissance and bombing missions. Leaders of industrialized nations quickly realized that mass production of consumer goods could just as easily be turned into the production of weapons of war.

World War I saw the development of a new kind of warfare in which men lived and died in rat-infested trenches, often knee-deep in mud.

When World War I broke out in the summer of 1914, the democracies of Europe prepared to display their might in what they believed would be a brief, glorious war. European powers had for centuries fought wars that served to realign the balance of power on the continent, and most leaders believed this war was no different. They had no idea what destruction lay ahead. This time it was Germany, under the leadership of the bellicose Kaiser Wilhelm II, that sought dominance. The German advance into France quickly ground to a halt, and five years of trench warfare followed.

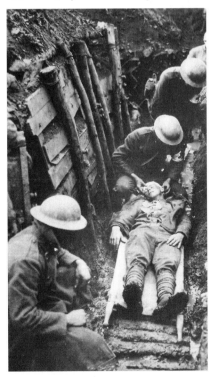

Protected from enemy gunfire by digging into the earth, men lived in rat-infested trenches, often knee-deep in mud. Daily living in the trenches was a horrifying affair, and when the soldiers crawled out of the earth and rushed through a desolate killing zone toward enemy positions in an attack, they passed their dead comrades' corpses and were ripped to bits by withering gunfire.

It soon became clear to the men, and more slowly to the generals, that technology had outstripped tactics. Machine guns and artillery pieces repulsed frontal assaults by foot soldiers and mounted cavalry again and again. The brutality and senselessness of World War I led to disillusionment among the soldiers and their leaders. This war, called "the War to End All War" by the writer H. G. Wells, finally ground to a halt in 1918.

"A Peace to End All Peace"

The Germans surrendered, but the war had nearly destroyed the combatant nations. Nearly an entire generation of European youths had been wiped out. And even the victorious countries teetered on the brink of financial ruin. In 1919 the belligerents of World War I met at the Trianon Palace of Versailles outside of Paris to sign a peace treaty. What happened at Versailles was no less a disaster than the war itself. The French, whose land soaked up most of the blood spilled during the war, insisted that Germany be made to pay for the war. The British and the French eagerly carved up the lands of the former Ottoman Empire, which had collapsed after its disastrous allegiance with Germany during the war. The Chinese, who had sent men to France to fight in the trenches, received a lasting insult when Germany's colonial holdings in China were awarded to Japan and other nations.

The final terms of the Treaty of Versailles resulted in the bankruptcy of Germany, the disillusionment of China with Western democracies, and the redrawing of the Middle East into borders that would ensure war there in the future. "After 'the war to end war,'" wrote British field marshal Earl Wavell, "they seem to have been pretty successful in Paris at making a 'Peace to end all Peace.'"[1]

Some historians have argued that the aftermath of World War I created the conditions that made it possible for modern dictators to thrive. The ruined economies of Europe fostered the rise of some; the haphazardly drawn borders guaranteed that old hatreds and rivalries would continue—and that dictators would be able to exploit them for their own gain.

Historian Charles L. Mee Jr. argued that the Treaty of Versailles was responsible for many of the conflicts of the twentieth century:

The failure of the diplomats of 1919—a failure that no one has since been able to repair, whose results we have lived with ever since—has been a terribly mixed legacy. The rise of Hitler, the Second World War, the riots and revolutions that plague a world without political order have been the cause of enormous bloodshed and suffering.[2]

Ideological Battles

One direct result of World War I was the triumph of Communism in Russia. The sacrifices demanded by the czar of his sprawling masses were resented by the vast number of Russian people. Communism promised a way out of the misery of being ruled by leaders unsympathetic with the aspirations of the common man. Its bold theories advocated the reorganization of society and offered opportunities to people who had none before.

Aside from the abolition of private property, Communism advocated international cooperation of workers in fomenting revolution

The signing of the Treaty of Versailles in 1919. Although it was meant to end war, the treaty paved the way for future conflicts and the rise of dictators in a number of nations.

against capitalists and their governments. For poor workers and farmers around the world, Communism seemed an attractive alternative. It offered them a way out of their own toiling; it offered them a chance to determine their own future. "Man's own social organization," wrote Communist theorist Friedrich Engels, "hitherto confronting him as a necessity imposed by nature and history, now becomes the result of his own free action."[3]

The choice was made by the people of Russia, where the Communists, led by Vladimir Ilich Lenin, established the Union of Soviet Socialist Republics (USSR) to create a nation ruled by workers. But running a Communist nation proved more difficult than establishing one. Nevertheless, the Soviet Union provided a guiding light for Communists all over the world who wished to establish Communist regimes in their own countries.

Another ideological movement that appeared after World War I was Fascism. Fascism, like Communism, appealed to people who were dissatisfied with their nation's political leadership and social organization, but the Fascists, rather than hoping to establish a revolutionary society, hoped to reestablish the past glories of their own countries. Fascism thrived through the promotion of myths of past national glory. In Germany, Adolf Hitler dreamed of restoring the tribal pride of the ancient German people; in Spain, Francisco Franco hoped to recapture the splendor of the Spanish imperial navy and to reestablish the supremacy of the Catholic Church and the Spanish monarchy.

As nationalist extremists, the Fascists hated international Communism. Fascists believed that Communism corroded the social fabric of their particular nations. The ideological conflict between Fascists and Communists erupted into a shooting war in Spain in 1939. The Spanish Civil War, provoked by a rebellion of Spanish military leaders under General Franco, drew the attention of the international community. The Soviets sent military aid and advisers to the forces loyal to Spain's elected government. The Loyalist ranks were also filled by volunteers from liberal democracies such as the United States, Great Britain, and France. On the opposite side, General Franco received aid, in the form of military machinery and troops, from the Fascist governments of Germany and Italy.

For a while it seemed that the Loyalists would win out in Spain. English novelist George Orwell, a volunteer for the Loyalist side, described the optimistic atmosphere of the Loyalists in the Spanish province of Catalonia during the early war years: "Above all there was a belief in the revolution and the future, a feeling of having suddenly emerged into an era of equality and freedom. Human beings were trying to behave as human beings and not as cogs in the capitalist machine."[4] But Orwell's optimism was short-lived. Franco sacked the Spanish capital in 1939 and established a Fascist government in Spain. That same year Hitler launched his blitzkrieg, or lightning war, against Poland, dooming the world to another global conflict.

Though Fascism suffered a mortal blow with the defeat of Hitler in 1945, Communism flourished in the postwar years. The Soviet Union under Stalin became a world power. China joined the Communist world in 1949, and in 1959 Cuba became the first Communist dictatorship established in the Western Hemisphere.

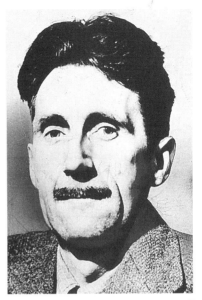

British novelist George Orwell joined the Loyalists in the fight against Franco.

As Communism spread in the years after World War II, Communist and non-Communist nations formed ideological blocs. These blocs embarked on an ideological battle known as the Cold War, which lasted for more than forty years. The Cold War world lived in constant fear of a third world war, one that would likely be fought with atomic weapons. The United States and the Soviet Union quickly found themselves engaged in a ruinously expensive arms race.

The Cold War was fought on many fronts, and often it flashed into hot war, as when the Americans faced Communist adversaries in Korea and Vietnam. More often, the United States and the USSR fought the Cold War by backing national leaders—often little more than armed thugs—who promised to promote the ideology favored by the respective superpower.

Throughout the twentieth century, dictators, both Communist and Fascist, caused enormous suffering. Their absolute powers resulted in the suppression of their citizens' rights and in a century of hot war and cold war. All of these dictators hoped to bring greatness to their countries but suffered in the end from the seduction of absolute power. Historian Hugh Trevor-Roper, one of the many scholars who have attempted to understand Hitler's madness, described the corrosive nature of dictatorship in *The Last Days of Hitler:*

Most historical dictators have passed through similar stages of development. Starting with revolutionary power, based on a revolutionary idea which happens to symbolize the mood of a people, they convert it into military power based on success; when the revolutionary premise is betrayed, and the success runs dry, they resort to naked power, based on political expedients and secret police; but since these are inadequate in the long run, the system collapses, or is overthrown. In theory, of course, revolutionary power can become respectable and traditional, and develop along orderly lines, as happened in the Roman Empire; but most of the great modern dictators—[England's Oliver] Cromwell, Napoleon, Hitler, [and Italy's Benito] Mussolini—went the other way; and the reason is, I believe, the ultimate inefficiency of dictatorial power, which causes success to run dry.[5]

The price of dictatorships in the twentieth century has been paid by common people. The ambitions of the people have been placed second to the ambitions of their leaders, and their voices have been drowned out by the blustering rants of these power-mongers. Dictators continue along this path even today. The populations of Cuba and Iraq, for example, are still ruled by absolute dictators, and their leaders continue along paths ruinous to the economies of their people. Though most people on Earth enjoy a higher standard of living today than they did a hundred years ago, dictatorships survive as living reminders of the dangers of absolute power. The century that began on such a hopeful note has left many hopes unfulfilled. "What a terrible disappointment," wrote British prime minister Winston Churchill, "the twentieth century has been."[6]

CHAPTER 2

Francisco Franco

Languishing in semi-exile as governor of the Spanish-controlled Canary Islands in 1936, a young general named Francisco Franco longed to return to Spain and stamp out the growing Socialist tendencies of the recently established Spanish Republic and its elected leader, President Manuel Azaña y Díaz. Franco thought that Azaña's electoral victory threatened everything he believed in, everything he thought to be good about Spain: the military, the Catholic Church, and the Spanish monarchy.

Franco devoted his entire life to advancement in the Spanish military, which had given members of his family their occupations for generations. Franco thought most highly of the navy, which in earlier centuries had brought back to Spain ships loaded with the riches of the far-flung Spanish empire. From his boyhood at the El Ferrol naval base in the extreme northwestern corner of Spain, Franco had heard the glorious tales from Spain's age of conquest and dreamed of a career at sea. But Franco also grew up with a sense of injured national pride from the defeat suffered by the royal navy in the Spanish-American War of 1898. Franco would spend most of his life trying to overcome this sense of humiliation.

The Little Soldier

On December 4, 1892, at El Ferrol naval base, a child was christened Francisco Paulino Hermenegildo Teódulo Franco Bahamonde. His father, a navy paymaster, was something of a local Don Juan, flirting with local women and spending much of the family's meager earnings on drink. As a child, Francisco took on the mournful character of his mother, who tolerated her husband's unfaithfulness and spent much of her time in prayer. At school, Francisco, a timid, small-statured boy, suffered the bullying of his classmates.

Francisco responded to the shame his father's philandering brought the family by increasing his devotion to the church.

Longing for a sense of order, he became a disciplined, solitary child and eagerly awaited the day when he could join Spain's navy. When his older brother Nicolas entered a Spanish naval academy, Francisco seethed with envy, longing for his turn. The navy, however, was not to be young Franco's future. The Spanish naval academy stopped taking recruits just before Francisco was eligible, so at age fifteen Francisco entered the Spanish army's military academy at Toledo. There, he assumed a stiff manner to compensate for his scrawny frame. To make himself appear older, he grew a pencil-thin mustache, which would be a trademark for the rest of his life. Determined to make the best of what he considered the "inferior" branch of the military, Francisco excelled in the rigid discipline of the army.

In addition to a sense of discipline, young Franco absorbed the reactionary creed of the Spanish military: love of the monarchy and a hatred of Spanish social reformers. Only dimly aware of the resentment the peasants and urban workers felt toward the privileged classes, Franco happily sang the praises of the monarchy, the military, and the church.

His small size once again spurred the criticism of fellow students and commanders. But to their taunts, Franco replied, "Whatever the strongest man here can do, Francisco Franco can also do."[7]

To put an end to the bullying, Franco fought back. On one occasion, when older students hid his books, Franco hurled a heavy candlestick at the head of another student. He rationalized this incident by arguing that "my dignity could not tolerate a joke like that repeated once too often."[8] His pluck made an impression on the authorities at school, however. Though never well liked by other students, he graduated with distinction and a commission as a second lieutenant.

Franco had looked forward to leaving his home and winning distinction in the Spanish army, so he fumed when he was posted to his hometown of El Ferrol. Franco found it

Francisco Franco (left), age fifteen, with his brother Nicolas.

no more exciting the second time around. Surrounded by an aging class of officers who whiled away their time discussing historic or imaginary battles, Franco longed for actual combat in which he could test his mettle and win promotion.

Into the Er Rif

A flare-up of rebellion in the Er Rif mountains of northern Morocco, then a Spanish protectorate, gave Franco just the chance he was hoping for, and he volunteered to serve with his country's colonial troops. With rocky hills, steep mountains, and frigid nights, the Er Rif is tough country. Er Rif tribesmen took advantage of the rugged terrain and waged a violent guerrilla war against the Spanish, scrambling through the hills and attacking Spanish outposts and patrols.

Franco had been sure that victory would be quick, and he was disappointed when Spanish troops suffered sharp defeats at the hands of the hill tribesmen of the Er Rif. The tribesmen had been organized and whipped into a frenzy by Abd el-Krim, a charismatic leader who tapped into the pride and religious fervor of his people. The Moors, as the inhabitants of northwestern Africa were called by Europeans, had occupied much of southern Spain during the Middle Ages and chafed under Spanish rule. For the Spanish army, the troublesome tribesmen recalled the insult of Spain's having been invaded centuries earlier by Moors. Spanish Morocco must be held, they determined, thinking of the past glories of the Reconquista, as Spain's eviction of the Moorish invaders was known.

Finding Spain's forces in Africa dispirited, Franco determined to add his own vigor to the fight. He volunteered for the most dangerous missions and soon had command of a troop of native Moroccan soldiers. The threat of mutiny was real, and Franco at first had to post guards at night to prevent assassination by his own troops. Within a short time, however, he molded these troops into a fierce and disciplined squad. His love for discipline and his toughness with his soldiers overshadowed his diminutive stature and squeaky voice, and though he was everywhere referred to as Franquito ("little Franco"), he won the respect of his superiors. Within three months of arriving in Morocco in 1912, Franco was promoted to first lieutenant and received awards for valor in battle.

Franco neither drank nor smoked and socialized little. In the field, he constantly surveyed the landscape and drilled his men even when there were no reports of nearby activity by Riffs, as the Er Rif

Franco as a cadet in the Spanish infantry.

mountain fighters were called. Unimaginative and solitary while off duty, Franco had a ruthless instinct for waging war and an insatiable appetite for promotion. Some cynical veterans scoffed at Franco's seriousness and attention to duty. "Sniffing at glory," one Spanish officer described Franco's ambition, "as he might have sniffed at a flower."[9]

Even Franco's rigid self-discipline could not protect him from every physical danger. In 1916 a Riff bullet brought down the young lieutenant. He returned to Spain, where he was awarded the rank of major—the youngest (at age twenty-four) in the Spanish army—by the king himself. Franco was establishing himself as a worthy member of the "Africa generation" of military men, who, unlike their inactive fellow officers in Spain, won quick promotion through combat. Franco later recorded in his diary that Africa was "the best, if not the only, practical school for the army."[10]

While Franco was recovering from his wound in Oviedo, a city near Spain's northern coast, he married Carmen Polo y Martinez, the daughter of an Oviedo wine merchant. Following quickly on the heels of the marriage was more good news. A seasoned veteran of the Africa campaigns, Colonel Millan Astray, dispatched a telegram to Franco offering him a command in the newly formed Spanish foreign legion in Morocco. Franco jumped at the chance to serve with Astray. A rakish, much-decorated figure in the battles with the Riffs, Astray drove his men mercilessly and demanded absolute obedience. A favorite saying of the colonel was "Down with intelligence: long live death."[11] Franco's job would once again be to hammer a group of rebellious, unprofessional soldiers into a disciplined fighting force.

The ragtag collection of adventurers, rascals, and criminals from Europe and North Africa gradually became infected with Franco's energy and discipline. When rebels attacked the city of Melilla, located on Morocco's northern coast, the legionnaires were sent to retake the city. The fierce fighting left many dead on both sides, but the city was retaken. The battle also provided Franco's first big break. Millan Astray fell in battle and died from a wound in the chest, leaving the Spanish foreign legion without a commander. With the death of his mentor, Franco was promoted to lieutenant colonel and assumed command of the foreign legion in 1923.

The Army Loses Support

While Franco and the other members of the "Africa generation" were winning fame through war in Morocco, a rift between the ruling classes and the Spanish masses was widening at home. Spain's fortunes had risen centuries earlier through its colonial holdings in the Americas and in the Pacific, but that wealth had flowed into the purses of wealthy merchants, the Catholic Church, and the king's treasury. The rich concentrated on building their treasure ships and overseas forts while Spanish peasants plowed the fields, reaping a subsistence living.

By the early part of the twentieth century, Spanish peasants and urban workers had begun to assert their political voice both through elections and through violence. Socialist and Communist theories, which advocated ownership of factories by the workers and a redistribution of land and other resources to the common people, had found their way to Spain. The success of the Russian Revolution of 1917 boosted the spirits of social reformers in Spain. A third political group, the Anarchists, who believed in the destruction of traditional authority and of all forms of government, joined the Socialists and Communists in fighting against the old bastions of power in Spain, namely the king, the rich, the military, and the church.

It seemed that the days of Spain's wealthy ruling class were numbered, although for a time the tide of reform was checked by the rise to power of the dictator Miguel Primo de Rivera y Orbaneja. For the conservatives in Spain, it was

Spanish dictator Miguel Primo de Rivera opposed social reform in his nation.

a relief that a strongman had stepped in to end what they saw as the leftist disease eating away at the Spanish state. Primo de Rivera viewed the war in Morocco as a drain on state finances. "Spain," he told Spanish officers in Morocco, "cannot continue to maintain her soldiers on these peaks, in these ravines and among these rocks which are costing her so dear, in blood and in gold. I think, therefore, that the moment has come to put an end to this." Franco replied with a fierce rebuttal: "This earth that we tread, Sir, is Spanish earth. . . . When we ask to continue with the war, to push on, it is not for our pleasure . . . it is because we are sure that Spain is in a position to dominate the zone placed under her protection and to impose her authority in Morocco."[12]

Though the words were sharp, Franco obeyed Primo de Rivera. When Franco returned from Morocco, he was rewarded with a promotion to brigadier general. He was but thirty-two years old and the youngest brigadier general in Europe. In just fifteen years of service in Africa, he had climbed the entire ladder of army advancement. Franco saw further opportunity, however, in Primo de Rivera's offer of command of Spain's military academy at Saragossa.

Franco's time as director of the military academy was a happy one. His wife gave birth to Carmencita, Franco's only child. Though he was resented by older generals whom he had leapt over for promotions and honors, life at the academy suited Franco. This time of calm was the lull before the storm, however.

In 1931, amid much violence, the reformers in Spain won a national election and used their newfound power to establish a government based on representation by freely elected officials. King Alfonso XIII, though seemingly dazed by events, delivered a graceful resignation to avoid civil war saying, "I am determined to have nothing to do with setting one of my countrymen against another in a fratricidal war."[13] The change in government was as swift as it was complete. As one of the king's men remarked, "Spain went to bed monarchist and woke up republican."[14]

The new government proved to be no friend of Spain's military. It closed the military academy at Saragossa and greatly reduced the military budget. Franco remained loyal at first to the new government, but he harbored secret ambitions to see the monarchy reestablished. Many other generals did not keep their ambitions secret. General José Sanjurjo, "the Lion of the Rif," for example, attempted to seize the government by force and was exiled to Portugal for his troubles. Franco waited, his ambitions and loyalties a secret to both his old comrades from the Er Rif and the new government in Madrid.

Though Franco had shown loyalty by not joining Sanjurjo's rebellion, the Republican government took no chances. Franco was restationed in the Balearic Islands in the Mediterranean, where he was safely out of the way. Exiling what the Republicans saw as their most dangerous foes did not end opposition to the government, however. Primo de Rivera's son, José Antonio, organized a political party called the Falange. The Falange was heavily influenced by Fascist ideas that were gaining favor in Italy and Germany and fought against left-wing political groups with political enforcers known as the Blueshirts. More direct confrontation lay ahead.

The new Republican government, wary of Franco, stationed him at remote outposts on the Balearic Islands in the Mediterranean.

José Primo de Rivera was courting Franco's support for a rebellion against the government, but Franco was assigned to the Canary Islands, where he was once more out of the way. Franco cut an inconspicuous figure as military governor of the islands. He swam in the pool with his wife and daughter and occasionally entertained military guests from Spanish Morocco or from the Spanish mainland. Watched closely by government security police, Franco appeared to be quietly caged.

Open Revolt

The battle between the left and right, between government supporters and antigovernment partisans, intensified. The violence increased as the Communists, Socialists, and Anarchists seized land and factories by force. The Republicans believed that the traditional hierarchy of the Catholic Church worked alongside the government to preserve the rich rulers of Spain. The Republicans vented their hatred against the Catholic Church by torching churches in many cities and towns. Just as the Republicans torched churches as symbols of a hated oppressor, they also beat and murdered political opponents, including priests. According to Spanish historian Edouard de Blaye, 160 churches were burnt between February 16 and June 15, 1936;

269 persons were assassinated, and 1,287 were wounded. Fighters for the left and the right machine-gunned each other in the streets of Madrid. Frequent strikes further paralyzed the country. Franco kept abreast of the growing chaos in Spain by reading newspapers and maintaining contact with military colleagues. As Spain lurched toward civil war, Franco saw his opportunity.

At dawn on July 19, 1936, an inconspicuous figure—thinly disguised by a hat and glasses—boarded the *Dragón Rapide,* a small plane that had been quietly chartered in London by a member of the Spanish military. The passenger, carrying only a small suitcase, presented himself to the English pilot with the simple words "I am General Franco" and told the pilot to avoid Spanish government aircraft. Without questions, the pilot flew Franco to Spanish Morocco, where he was met by members of Spain's colonial army and his old commands, the Spanish foreign legion and the Regulares.

Franco's flight to Morocco was part of a detailed plan. Earlier that morning, Franco had transmitted a message from the Canary Islands to Spain calling for the uprising of "whoever feels a holy love of Spain."[15] His pronouncement signaled the beginning of a military revolt against the elected government of Spain. This uprising, called El Alzamiento in Spanish, plunged Spain into a four-year civil war. Franco would soon be thrust into leadership of the rebels.

The original leader of the conspirators was José Sanjurjo, but he died in a plane crash only two months after the beginning of the uprising. Franco assumed the role of commander in chief, and by October of that year he was appointed head of state and generalissimo of the Nationalist armies. Under Franco, the rebel Nationalist armies achieved considerable success in the early months of the war. They quickly seized power in the cities of Cadíz, Saragossa, Seville, and Burgos while the government forces held Madrid, Barcelona, Bilbao, and Valencia. Spain was divided into two parts, with the Nationalist territories lying in the north and the west, and the government remaining in control of the capital and much of the southeast of Spain, the eastern coast, and the northwestern province of Catalonia.

Franco's objective in leading the rebellion was to restore the monarchy, defeat the anticlerical Republican government, and establish "a military dictatorship to last as long as necessary to restore order and the national economy."[16] He had the support of the church and most of the rich landowners of Spain as well as most of the military and the heavily armed *guardia civil,* or civilian police.

Franco's Spain

Although much of Spain's military backed Franco, the government retained some loyal troops. In addition, citizens formed local militias. Both sides also received help from other countries. The United States and the democracies of Europe stayed neutral in the conflict, but many citizens from those countries volunteered to fight against Fascism in Spain. These foreigners formed the International Brigade, which eventually received considerable assistance from the Soviet Union.

The progovernment forces, however, were at the outset of the insurrection poorly organized and suffered heavy losses. Moreover, their meager supply of manpower and weapons could not compete with the generous support Franco received from the Fascist dictators of Italy and Germany.

The morning Franco boarded the *Dragón Rapide*, he had wired Italy's Fascist dictator Benito Mussolini requesting support; similar pleas to Germany's Adolf Hitler followed soon after. By November 1936 both dictators had officially recognized Franco's

Fascist Italian dictator Benito Mussolini (pictured) supported Franco by sending Italian troops to fight against the Spanish Loyalists.

regime. Troops and supplies followed. From Mussolini, Franco received more than fifty thousand Italian "volunteers," trained soldiers who fought side by side with the Nationalists.

Hitler sent "volunteers" (most of whom were soldiers who were ordered to serve in Spain) and German planes, which he was eager to test in combat. As they flew missions in Spanish skies, the German pilots perfected their dive-bombing techniques, contributing considerably to Franco's victory. Both civilian and military targets were attacked, representing the first instance of the indiscriminate bombing of cities during an air war.

The rebels were helped by both support from abroad and dissension among the Loyalists. In the final days of the war, disagreements over ideology and the future of Spain broke out among the government forces. To make matters worse, the Russians began to withdraw aid from the government. Resistance to Franco's armies crumbled, and the Spanish capital surrendered to rebel forces on March 28, 1939.

The war had been a costly affair. Nearly three-quarters of a million people died in the fighting; to that number Franco added about 250,000 Republicans who were killed after the war in a great purge of suspected leftist sympathizers.

The Caudillo

Some Spaniards, no doubt, were pleased with the war's outcome. Franco had restored order, returned the king to his throne, and reinstated the ancient privileges of the Catholic Church. The pope sent his blessings and congratulations from Rome. "Lifting up our heart to the Lord," Pope Pius XII wrote, "we rejoice with Your Excellency in the victory, so greatly desired, of Catholic Spain. We pray that your most beloved country, with peace attained, may take up again with new vigor the ancient Christian traditions which made her so great."[17]

Hitler and Mussolini also sent congratulations and invited Franco to join them in the brewing European conflict that would soon turn into World War II. Much to their chagrin, Franco declined, choosing neutrality for Spain. Although he sent volunteers to the Russian front to fight for Hitler, Franco knew that his country had suffered enough war. Ironically, while his fellow dictators plunged the rest of Europe into war, Franco initiated the longest peace in Spanish history.

Yet Franco's dictatorship and his ideological sympathy with the Axis powers during World War II left Spain isolated after the Allied defeat of Germany and Italy. The financial reconstruction of the defeated nations, sponsored by the American government, was not offered to Spain. And while Europe enjoyed prosperity and democracy in the postwar years, Spain stood aloof—a poor country with a totalitarian government. Franco resisted all efforts to modernize his country. Indeed, Spain would stand still under his leadership for nearly thirty more years. Franco fundamentally distrusted change. Though he encouraged industrial projects, the Spanish economy remained backward. A ban on strikes by workers was enforced with violence. Other aspects of society, such as

Franco meets the archbishop of Seville. Franco supported Catholicism and the clergy; the pope, in turn, endorsed Franco's dictatorship.

Franco poses with matadors at a bullfight. Toward the end of his rule, Franco increasingly spent his time on leisure pursuits including hunting and fishing.

education, were tightly controlled; Franco reduced the salaries of educators and quashed intellectual debate. Likewise, the press became an organ of the state rather than a forum for the free exchange of ideas.

Only rarely did Franco attempt to break Spain's diplomatic isolation. In 1953 Franco signed a cooperation pact making Spain a member of the North Atlantic Treaty Organization (NATO), and in 1956 Franco granted independence to the Spanish protectorate of Morocco and received the Moroccan king, Muhammad V, as a gesture of friendship. The intensifying Cold War between the United States and the Soviet Union made Franco, the fanatical anticommunist, a little more palatable to the Western democracies. Nevertheless, at the 1957 signing of the Treaty of Rome, which established a plan for the European Economic Community, Spain was excluded. Franco remained isolationist to his last years, controlling the government in the autocratic manner of the caudillo, as Spain's dictator was called.

As the years went by, Franco devoted much of his time to his family and to leisure pursuits. Franco enjoyed taking long holidays. He hunted and fished and played at being a gentleman. His freedom and carefree appearance were in marked contrast to the deep economic problems of most Spaniards and to their lack of political voice. Spain's situation seemed not to concern him, however. In fact, his grasp of reality was sometimes questioned. As he told the Cortes, the Spanish legislature, in 1961, "Never has Spain known a state more legitimate, popular and representative."[18]

Though Franco claimed late in his life that "providence will provide for Spain when I go,"[19] he made his desires known and in 1970 presented to the Cortes Prince Juan Carlos as his successor. His final years were spent in and out of the hospital. On November 20, 1975, after the last in a series of heart attacks, Francisco Franco died at El Pardo.

Franco had indeed managed to keep modernization and progress at Spain's borders. In traditional manner, he placed the financial burdens of his policies on the peasants and poor urban workers. Franco's final wish, that all would continue as he had left it, was not fulfilled. Beginning with his death in 1975, Spain sped headlong into a remarkable period of development and prosperity. Today, it is a strong partner in the European Economic Community and a thriving democracy.

CHAPTER 3

Adolf Hitler

Adolf Hitler was the undisputed leader, or führer, of Nazi Germany. World War II, which drew combatants from around the globe and lasted from 1939 to 1945, was largely Hitler's war. Hitler's dreams for Germany had no limits, and by his own will, he launched a war that nearly ruined Germany. "Hitler," wrote German army commander Walther von Brauchitsch, "was the fate of Germany and this fate could not be stayed."[20]

A Budding Nationalist

Little in Hitler's early life points to the hypnotic powers that he would hold over the German people as an adult. In fact, his childhood in Linz, the capital of Upper Austria, was far from extraordinary. Adolf Hitler was born in the Austrian town of Braunau-on-the-Inn on April 20, 1889, across the border from

Germany. His father, Alois Hitler, was an obscure Austrian customs official, and his mother, Klara Poelzl, was a domestic servant.

At the time of Hitler's birth, Austria was still part of the Austro-Hungarian Empire. As Hitler grew older, he developed an intense hatred of Austria's union with Hungary, which united the Germanic people of Austria with the non-German, Slavic people of Hungary. The site of Hitler's birth, on the border of Germany, heightened his awareness of the division between the two Germanic states of Austria and Germany, which he believed should be united.

Little in Hitler's early life suggested that he would one day be the undisputed dictator of Germany.

"Today it seems to me providential," Hitler wrote in his autobiography, *Mein Kampf,* "that fate should have chosen Braunau am Inn as my birthplace. For this little town lies on the boundary between two German states which we of the younger generation at least have made it our life-work to reunite by every means at our disposal."[21] Although Hitler romanticized his past in *Mein Kampf,* suggesting that as a youth he harbored grand ambitions, his childhood was one that showed little direction.

Adolf Hitler attended school in the town of Linz, where he was a lackluster student. His father hoped that Adolf would eventually gain stable employment as a civil servant like himself. But the boy resisted his father's attempts to control his future, for young Adolf wanted to become an artist. Hitler left school early and made his way to Vienna, the Austrian capital, to pursue his dreams of becoming an artist.

Days of Frustration

In Vienna, Hitler spent his days eking out a living as a painter of postcards and working at other small artistic projects. His life was dreary and solitary. He lived in the poorer neighborhoods, moving from flophouse to flophouse. His days were filled with brooding and with dabbling with his paintbrushes. At night he spent his time reading, and sometimes he hovered outside the Vienna opera house, listening to the mythic operas of Richard Wagner, his favorite composer. Wagner's music echoed of Germanic pride, and Hitler was spellbound.

Hitler resented the fact that he could not afford to attend the operas he loved, but the crowning insult of Hitler's life in Vienna was his failure to gain entry to the prestigious Academy of Art. The bitterness over his own failures hardened into a hatred of the world around him.

Although Vienna was in many ways a cosmopolitan world, full of grand buildings and pleasure-loving people, it was also a place where anti-Semitism flourished. As Hitler's bitterness deepened and his German nationalism intensified, he found a single peg on which to hang his most virulent hatreds: the Jews. While Hitler, ill fed and ill clothed, scraped his pennies together to buy lunch, he saw Jews leading prosperous lives as bankers, businessmen, and artists. His jealousy and frustration fed his hatred. "This was the time," wrote Hitler, "in which the greatest change I was ever to experience took place. From a feeble cosmopolite I had turned into a fanatical anti-Semite."[22]

The Vienna opera house, where as a young man Hitler listened to the operas of Wagner. Hitler was captivated by the operas' celebration of German culture.

The Austrian Corporal

Hitler's aimless life in Vienna, which he later called the saddest period of his life, came to a sudden end with the outbreak of World War I. The Austro-Hungarian Empire had joined the German kaiser (emperor) in a bid for greater influence on the European continent.

The kaiser, Wilhelm II, had long resented Britain's influence in Europe and its domination of the world's oceans. Seeing an opportunity to build his country's influence, he ordered the invasion of France.

The outbreak of war was greeted with enthusiasm by many Germans and Austrians. They believed that they could win prestige for the German people through war. Among those who clamored for war in the summer of 1914 was Adolf Hitler, who crossed the German border into Bavaria and joined the army. Hitler, small in stature and with an unhealthy pallor, took a boyish pride in his German uniform and threw himself wholeheartedly into his new role.

Hitler reveled in every moment of the grisly war that ensued. Seeing the German army in action heightened his patriotism and his belief in the virtues of war: discipline, bravery, and authoritarianism. He served as a corporal for four years with his Bavarian regiment and was twice decorated with the Iron Cross, Germany's highest military medal.

It was in the final months of the war that Hitler was injured in a British mustard-gas attack. Stretcher bearers carried Corporal Hitler out of the mud, the poisonous haze of gas, and the din of war. The gas, which is highly caustic, had burned his eyes, temporarily blinding him. As he lay in the hospital, his eyes wrapped in bandages, he learned that the war had ground to a halt and that Germany, on the brink of bankruptcy, had surrendered.

Into the Fray

Germany's surrender plunged Hitler into the depths of misery. All the camaraderie and pride he had found in military life had come to nothing. Hitler felt that Germany's surrender was a national disaster, and all around him he saw the suffering of the German people as the economy crumbled under the strain of five years of war.

The Treaty of Versailles, which formally ended the war in 1919, levied heavy financial burdens on Germany. The treaty was not so much a design for future peace as it was a final punishment for the Germans, who had, after all, started the war. Under the treaty's

terms, France took Alsace-Lorraine, an area on the border between France and Germany that the two nations had long fought over; German Prussia was also broken up, its lands distributed to Poland and Czechoslovakia. The Rhineland, the part of Germany west of the Rhine River, was demilitarized, preventing Germany from any military defense against the French. Not only did Germany lose part of its own territory under the Treaty of Versailles, but it also lost its colonial possessions in Asia and Africa. Even a British historian later wrote

Hitler served for four years as a corporal in the German army during World War I.

that the Treaty of Versailles was, for Germany, a "humiliation without precedent or equal in modern history."[23]

Not only was Hitler demoralized by the treaty terms, but he also feared the rise of Communism in Germany. After the war, Germany swarmed with antigovernment agitators of all kinds, and the Communists promised the German people a way out of their misery through social revolution and the destruction of German institutions like the Reichstag, or German legislature, and the German army. For Hilter, the Communists offered Germany only a different path to ruin. "[Germany's] misfortunes," British prime minister Winston Churchill later wrote about Hitler, "did not lead him into Communist ranks. By an honorable inversion he cherished all the more an abnormal sense of racial loyalty and a fervent and mystic admiration for Germany and the German people."[24]

Discharged from the hospital shortly after the war's end, Hitler joined the German Workers' Party, later called the National Socialist or Nazi Party, and fought as a member of this ultranationalist organization against the terms of the Treaty of Versailles. Now the anti-Semitism from his years in Vienna boiled to the surface. Hitler came to believe that not only the Allied powers had ruined Germany but also the Jews, whom he accused of profiteering and in-

A photo dated September 2, 1923, shows Hitler at a political rally. Two months later, he felt that the Nazis were strong enough to stage what has become known as the Beer Hall Putsch.

The private army of the Nazi Party was known as the Sturmabteilung ("storm troopers"), or SA. Here, members of the SA harass German Jews.

triguing behind the scenes during the war. In Hitler's imagination, the Jews were in an evil alliance with international Communism.

Far from being the aimless dreamer he had been in Vienna, Hitler emerged from World War I as a fully politicized, virulently energetic Nazi Party leader. He believed that the German postwar republic, established after the kaiser fled Germany at the end of the war, betrayed Germany's natural superiority. His beliefs were bolstered above all by a mystical belief in the superiority of the German people.

Hitler found supporters for the Nazi Party in Munich, where many dissatisfied former soldiers fumed with resentment over the Versailles treaty. Many of these soldiers had refused to give up their uniforms at the end of the war, and they agitated against the government in Berlin. Hitler showed a talent for public speaking and whipped these discontented German soldiers into a frenzy of hatred for the countries that had imposed the Versailles treaty on Germany. With spellbinding oratory, Hitler also spoke of what he considered the menace of Jews and Slavs.

Hitler's genius for rabble-rousing and propaganda swelled the ranks of the Nazi Party. German Communists reacted by trying to break up Nazi rallies, and street battles resulted. To protect their members, the Nazis enlisted squads of thugs. Ernst Röhm, one of the earliest members of the Nazi Party, organized these toughs into a private army, called the SA (Sturmabteilung, or "storm troopers"), complete with military uniforms. The storm troopers terrorized the Communists in turn. They targeted not only their political opponents but also Jews and other ethnic minorities.

By 1923 Hitler believed that the Nazi Party was strong enough to seize power in Germany. The SA sprang into action. At a political rally held at one of Munich's beer halls, the Nazis declared open revolt. After a night of rioting, the insurrection was suppressed by the police, and the movement's leaders were arrested. The Beer Hall Putsch, as the insurrection was later called, landed Hitler in prison.

At his trial, Hitler was unrepentant. "You may pronounce us guilty a thousand times over," Hitler told the judge before sentencing, "but the goddess of the eternal court of history will smile and tear to tatters the brief of the state prosecutor and the sentence of this court."[25]

In prison, Hitler was treated like an honored guest. He served only thirteen months of his five-year sentence, and he used the peace and quiet of his cell to write *Mein Kampf (My Struggle)*, his autobiography and guide for the future action of the Nazi Party. In *Mein Kampf*, Hitler reveals all of the frustrations and hatreds that would one day plunge Germany into World War II. "For years," writes historian Konrad Heiden, "*Mein Kampf* stood as proof of the blindness and complacency of the world. For in its pages Hitler announced—long before he came to power—a program of blood and terror in self-revelation of such overwhelming frankness that few among its readers had the courage to believe it."[26]

The Führer

The failure of the Beer Hall Putsch convinced Hitler that the Nazis would have to win power by legal means. It was not that Hitler believed in elections, but he thought that success would have to come through the channels of the established government. Hitler spent the years after his release from prison building up the party. The moody, brooding firebrand could also be seen during this time hiking through the mountains in native Bavarian garb: knee-high woolen socks, suspendered shorts, and a loden jacket.

Hitler's costume was part of the myth of the rugged German: an individual tied to the land and uncorrupted by the evil influence of the cities, which were supposedly full of foreign influences and money-grubbing businessmen. Through the party newspaper, the *Popular Observer,* the Nazis continued to pump out propaganda to the German people, gaining support for their venomous ideas. The scheme worked. In the 1930 elections, the Nazi Party received 6.5 million votes and was the second-largest party in Germany. Two years later, it won a majority of seats in Germany's legislature, the Reichstag. The führer was nearing his day.

Events outside Germany played into the Nazis' hands. The depression that swept the world after the New York stock market crash of 1929 bitterly impacted the German economy. Inflation, already preposterously high in Germany, reached devastating heights. The German currency, the mark, lost all value. Its value against the dollar reached a million to one, and the German people could hardly afford the barest of necessities. Under such conditions, savings accounts of the middle classes were wiped out entirely, adding to the discontent.

A master of propaganda, Hitler quickly gained the support of the German people. By 1932, the Nazi Party held a majority of seats in the Reichstag.

Germany's economic ruin paved the way for Hitler's triumph. Following the elections in 1932 that proved Hitler's popularity, Germany's president, Paul von Hindenburg, was forced to invite Hitler to assume the office of chancellor, hoping that his subordinates would check his worst excesses. By legal means, Hitler took the helm of the German republic with the determination to restore the historical glories of his people. "It is almost like a dream," wrote Joseph Goebbels, the chief propagandist of the Nazi Party. "The new Reich has been born. Fourteen years of hard work have been crowned with victory. The German revolution has begun!"[27]

Just weeks later Hitler was presented with a wonderful opportunity when the Reichstag was destroyed by fire. The fire was blamed on a Dutch Communist named Marianus van de Lubbe, but it may have been set by the Nazis. In any case, Hitler used the Reichstag fire as an excuse to widen his dictatorial powers. Brushing aside the constitution, he outlawed political opposition and gave himself sweeping powers to crush opponents with force.

Hitler is sworn in as chancellor on January 30, 1933. Once in office, Hitler began to solidify his control by outlawing political opposition.

Having smothered threats from outside the Nazi Party, Hitler then turned on his own ranks. Ernst Röhm, the leader of the storm troopers, was feared and hated by the German military establishment, whose loyalty Hitler needed to solidify in order to rule as dictator. On June 29, 1934, Hitler ordered the execution of Röhm and his chief supporters. Hitler used this "Night of Long Knives" to stab his oldest friends in the back. His ruthlessness, however, won him the support of the German general staff.

Hitler began to rebuild the army, which had been dismantled following World War I. In violation of the Treaty of Versailles, he reinstituted the military draft. He took the added step of having all recruits swear an oath of loyalty directly to their führer. The German military would now be under the personal leadership of Adolf Hitler.

In addition to gaining the sworn loyalty of the military, Hitler used propaganda and intimidation to win the support of 90 percent of the German people. He proclaimed his new government the Third Reich, which, he claimed, would last for a thousand years. Little concerned with domestic affairs, Hitler now set out on his grand plan, spelled out in *Mein Kampf,* of expanding German power abroad.

Lightning War

Hitler set about preparing his nation for war. He remilitarized the Rhineland, near the border of France, and ordered German industry to begin building arms. While war loomed, other European powers, such as England, France, and Russia, grasped at Hilter's promises. Anxious to avoid war, they signed nonaggression treaties with Germany. Europe's leaders chose to appease Hitler's demands that Germany be allowed to take over first Austria and then a portion of Czechoslovakia known as the Sudetenland. The Anschluss, as Germany's peaceful union with Austria was called, fulfilled Hitler's boyhood dream of uniting the German-speaking people into a single state. Hitler's goal in expanding the territory of Germany was to gain what he called *Lebensraum,* or "living space," for the German people. He would pursue this goal even if it meant war.

In September 1939 Hitler leveled the power of the Wehrmacht, the German army, on neighboring Poland, opening World War II. The French and British had pledged to support Poland against any German aggression, and not even those favoring appeasement could deny their national pledge to the Poles. The Allied powers were unprepared for war, and as they scrambled to prepare themselves for the second great conflict with Germany in the twentieth century, Polish resistance collapsed in less than four weeks.

Hitler danced a jig in Berlin. He had deceived the countries of Europe and the Soviet Union into believing that he had only limited ambitions. In fact, Hitler wanted nothing short of total victory in Europe and the subjugation of Russia. "Adolf Hitler," writes historian William L. Shirer, "is probably the last of the great adventurer-conquerors in the tradition of Alexander, Caesar and Napoleon, and the Third Reich the last of the empires which set out on the path taken earlier by France, Rome and Macedonia."[28]

The French scrambled in desperation to prepare for a German attack. True to the maxim that generals are always fighting the last war, the French had constructed a series of fortifications, called the Maginot Line, to protect the border from another German invasion. The heavily fortified entrenchments were impregnable and would probably have repelled a German advance had the Germans used the same tactics as they had in World War I. But Hitler was not fighting the last war.

Instead, he launched a new kind of war, a blitzkrieg, or "lightning war." Armored divisions led the assault with frightening speed and mobility. Climbing through a pass in the Ardennes for-

Hitler's blitzkrieg brought so much new territory under German control that the nation's troops were eventually spread too thin to successfully defend against counterattack.

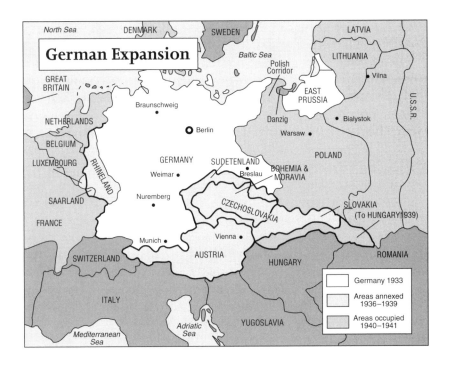

German Expansion

North Sea · DENMARK · SWEDEN · LATVIA · Baltic Sea · LITHUANIA · Polish Corridor · GREAT BRITAIN · Vilna · EAST PRUSSIA · U.S.S.R. · Braunschweig · Danzig · Bialystok · NETHERLANDS · Berlin · Warsaw · BELGIUM · POLAND · LUXEMBOURG · GERMANY · SUDETENLAND · BOHEMIA & MORAVIA · RHINELAND · Weimar · Breslau · SAARLAND · Nuremberg · CZECHOSLOVAKIA · SLOVAKIA (To HUNGARY 1939) · FRANCE · Munich · Vienna · AUSTRIA · ROMANIA · SWITZERLAND · HUNGARY · ITALY · Adriatic Sea · YUGOSLAVIA · Mediterranean Sea

Germany 1933
Areas annexed 1936–1939
Areas occupied 1940–1941

est, which lies between Belgium and France, the German blitzkrieg circled around the northernmost tip of the Maginot Line, leaving behind the massive earthworks, fixed, impregnable, and useless. Paris fell to the Nazi advance within seven weeks. Other European countries soon fell victim to similar assaults. Norway, Denmark, Belgium, the Netherlands, Yugoslavia, Greece, and Russia west of the Don River all fell to the advancing Germans. Hitler was on the verge of extinguishing all opposition in Europe. Only the British, protected in their island nation by the Royal Air Force and the Royal Navy, withstood the German advance.

The success of Hitler's lightning war surprised even the führer himself. The Germans found themselves occupying the greater part of Europe and fighting the Russians to the east along a two thousand-mile front. On the Russian front, the Germans won battles at enormous costs in manpower and machinery. The British and the Americans—who entered the war in 1941 after the Japanese bombed the American naval base at Pearl Harbor, Hawaii—further challenged Hitler's Wehrmacht by invading North Africa, where they battled the German Afrika Korps.

As the war ground on, some German generals felt that the army was overextended, that a war fought over such a vast area could only ruin the nation. By 1944 the Allies proved the German doubters right. North Africa had been retaken; the German advance in Russia had ground to a halt; and the Allied powers, on June 6, 1944, invaded France from the beaches of Normandy.

The more levelheaded German commanders, watching the destruction of their beloved German army, plotted against Hitler. On July 20, 1944, Colonel Claus von Stauffenberg placed a bomb, hidden in a briefcase, in Hitler's headquarters in East Prussia. Hitler's luck held, however. The explosion left the führer dazed but only slightly injured. The result was that Hitler tightened his grip on the military and pressed his war with renewed zeal.

In many ways Hitler was directly responsible for at least the initial successes of the German war effort. "Hitler's military talents were not really contemptible," writes British historian Hugh Trevor-Roper. "The extent of his knowledge, and his amazing grasp of detail, have been universally, if sometimes reluctantly, admitted; his will-power, which ultimately doomed Germany, sometimes achieved results which the professional generals, on purely logistical grounds, thought impossible."[29] The führer's willpower was not enough, in the end, to accomplish his grand schemes.

The End of a Dream

As the Allied powers closed in on Germany, Hitler ordered one last-ditch battle in the Ardennes. The Battle of the Bulge was Hitler's last gamble. His troops struck with the same ferocity that they exhibited in the blitzkrieg against France at the start of the war. But Allied bombing runs, which now ran around the clock, had decimated the German military machine. Supplies ran short, and recruiting fell miserably short of the manpower needed to defend the homeland. The Allies dealt Germany one more defeat in the Battle of the Bulge; the gamble had failed.

As the Allies approached the German capital, the führer, cornered in the rubble of Berlin, directed the war effort from a fortified bunker. His war, however, had been lost. According to Trevor-Roper, who marched into Berlin in 1945 with the British army,

> Hitler was still there, still the central figure, still the ultimate authority; but a Chinese wall separated him from the outer world of reality. He listened not to other voices, but to echoes of his own; for none of the surviving courtiers dared to speak, or even know the truth. He still interested himself in every detail, still moved armies by battalions and regiments; but it was on an imaginary battlefield.[30]

Hitler prepared for the end. He appointed a successor for a government that had already failed. Then, on April 29, 1945, he mar-

Concentration camp prisoners who were not sent immediately to the gas chambers were starved, beaten, and forced into slave labor.

ried Eva Braun, his longtime mistress. The following day the couple committed suicide. Whether they took their lives by poison or by gunshot is uncertain.

By committing suicide, Hitler evaded the Allies' noose. What Allied soldiers did find when they closed in on Hitler were the horrors of the death camps. The tales of these giant factories of death had been largely disbelieved. But the American, British, and French forces that advanced from the west came upon one grisly crematorium after another: Buchenwald, Dachau, and Bergen-Belsen. The Russians, advancing in the east, discovered Majdanek and Auschwitz.

Battle-hardened soldiers looked in horror at the rows of emaciated bodies, starved and beaten to death. They found the crematoriums and gas chambers where the Nazis disposed of Europe's Jews, along with others Hitler deemed "undesirable"—Slavs, Gypsies, Communists, and the disabled—without having to expend bullets that could be used against the Allies. Though Hitler called his Third Reich the Thousand-Year Reich, it lasted only twelve years and four months. Hitler's madness was at an end, and the world was left to look on his handiwork with utter disbelief.

CHAPTER 4

Joseph Stalin

During World War II British prime minister Winston Churchill quipped that he would make a deal with the devil to defeat Germany. The "devil" that Churchill was referring to was Joseph Stalin, the supreme leader of Communist Russia and one of the most brutal dictators in the history of civilization.

During his years as the leader of the Union of Soviet Socialist Republics, Stalin transformed an agrarian nation into a modern industrial country. But he did this by imposing tremendous suffering on the people of Russia.

In Czarist Russia

Stalin was born Iosif Vissarionovich Dzhugashvili on December 21, 1879. His birthplace was the town of Gori in the province of Georgia, which lies along the eastern edge of the Black Sea in the Caucasus Mountains.

As a child Stalin was called Soso, which is Georgian for "Joseph." He lived with his family in a small hovel on the southern slopes of the Caucasus. Gori was a remote outpost in the Russian czar's realm. In the countryside around his parent's tiny home, rivers rushed through the mountain passes. If he looked up toward the mountains, Soso could see the ruins of a fortress built by a Georgian feudal prince.

Georgia at that time was still a feudal place. His parents had been liberated from serfdom when they were children, but life continued much the same as it had for centuries. Soso's father, Vissarion, worked as a cobbler, and his mother, Yekaterina, as a washerwoman and domestic servant in richer households.

Vissarion was often drunk, and in his violent drunken rages, he often beat Soso. Soso resented his father and early in life developed a rebellious streak. Although his father was brutal, his mother was kind, and the small, wiry child found some solace in his mother's devotion to him. She wanted above all for Soselo, "Little Soso," ordination in the priesthood.

At school, Soso learned Russian, although for the rest of his life he would speak it with a strong Georgian accent. The short dark-

Stalin was born on December 21, 1879, in this house in Gori, Georgia, then part of czarist Russia.

haired Georgian with the pockmarked face—the result of a childhood skin disease—was a serious student, and his good grades at Gori won him a stipend to attend the theological seminary in Tbilisi, the capital of Georgia. His mother hoped that he would finish and enter the priesthood, but Stalin eventually came to believe that religion was nothing more than an ancient superstition.

The Making of a Revolutionary

At night at the seminary, he would meet with other students to discuss the writings of Karl Marx, who became known as "the Intellectual Father of Communism." Marx believed that religion was the opiate of the masses, a tool used by the established authorities to keep common people toiling away unquestioningly. They were duped, said Marx, into believing that they would find a better life after death in the heavens above.

Stalin agreed with Marx's view of religion. So, too, did Stalin find inspiration in Marx's belief that only through revolution could the common people stand up for their rights. These ideas and the books that preached them were forbidden in the Tbilisi seminary school, but Stalin hid the books around the school and read them whenever he could.

Karl Marx, the "Father of Communism" and inspiration to a teenage Stalin.

The rebellious Georgian had nursed a hatred for authority and cared little what the priests thought. "Since all people of authority over others," wrote a fellow seminary student about Stalin, "seemed to be like his father, there . . . rose in him a vengeful feeling against all standing above him."[31] Stalin's antireligious beliefs eventually came to the attention of his teachers, and in the spring of 1899 Stalin was expelled from the seminary. The nineteen-year-old rebel left behind his mother's dreams for him and set out to find a place in the new order of social revolutionaries that was growing in Russia.

Stalin found a menial job at the Tbilisi astronomical observatory, but he spent most of his time meeting with members of the Tbilisi branch of the Russian Social Democratic Party, an illegal revolutionary organization. He quickly proved himself to his comrades by drawing crowds to protests and rallies and injecting the movement with new energy.

Marx's teachings had spread through Russia, attracting many people who were shut out of the benefits enjoyed by the ruling classes. Marx taught that society would be transformed by the organization of industrial workers into a political unit. Russia at that time was just becoming industrialized, and Communism provided a new belief system for disillusioned workers who slaved thanklessly in the nation's mills and factories. "It is difficult to describe the process," Stalin said about the growth of Communism. "First one becomes convinced that existing conditions are wrong and unjust. Then one resolves to do the best one can to remedy them."[32]

Stalin took over the propaganda machine for the local Communist organizations and became a frequent speaker at their rallies. Meanwhile, the czar's police forces kept the revolutionaries in constant fear of imprisonment. In March 1902, for example, Stalin helped organize a demonstration of two thousand workers in the port city of Batum (modern-day Batumi), on the Black Sea coast. The marchers were met by armed police officers and cavalrymen, who opened fire on the illegal gathering. Fifteen demonstrators were killed and fifty-four were wounded. Stalin was not there to witness the carnage: He had slipped out sometime before the shooting started.

The following year, however, Stalin was not so lucky. The czar's police captured the young revolutionary and exiled him to Siberia, the vast frozen wasteland in eastern Russia that served as a prison for the czar's enemies. The icy temperatures and shortage of food made for hard living. But security was lax, and Stalin made his way back to Georgia.

Life as an Outlaw

Stalin would be exiled to Siberia six times, spending a total of eight and a half years there. Each time, Stalin escaped, a fact that led some to believe that he was actually an agent of the government. This charge has never been proven, however.

While secretly living in his mother's house after one escape from Siberia, Stalin married Ekaterina Svanidze, or "Keke" as she was called. Shortly after, she bore Stalin a son, Yakov. Their married life was short-lived, and Keke died of tuberculosis soon after the boy's birth. Stalin left Yakov with relatives so that he could carry on his struggle against the czar.

During these early years of

As a young man, Joseph Stalin devoted himself to revolution.

revolutionary activity, Stalin learned about a remarkable Russian exile living in Switzerland. This was Vladimir Ilich Lenin, a follower of Marxism and a principal leader of the Russian Communists. The two met for the first time shortly afterwards at a political conference in Finland, and Stalin thought he saw a true leader in Lenin.

Lenin, with his short stature, hairless head, and goatee, looked more like a university professor than a revolutionary. And, indeed, he was a remarkable scholar and a voracious reader. But Lenin's

Vladimir Ilich Lenin, Russian Communist and leader of the Bolsheviks, advocated a violent overthrow of the monarchy by the working class.

writings revealed a belief in violent revolution. Lenin became the leader of the fiercest revolutionary group—the Bolsheviks (which means "the Majority" in Russian). The Bolsheviks advocated armed struggle to overthrow the Russian monarchy and the bourgeoisie, or middle classes that engaged in trade and business. The second great faction of Russian revolutionaries, the Mensheviks ("the Minority"), believed in peaceful struggle. Although the two factions were working together, their alliance was an uneasy one.

As Stalin rose in the Bolshevik ranks, he revealed two traits that would mark his leadership for the rest of his life. He exhibited an extraordinary knack for political maneuvering and a ruthless willingness to use violence to achieve his goals. Stalin organized armed parties of bandits to rob banks, assassinate opposition, and carry out terrorist bombings against members of the czar's government. Lenin did not always know the details of Stalin's thuggery, but he knew that Stalin could be trusted to organize men and get things accomplished. Stalin felt at home moving through the lawless underworld of Russia's cities.

At this time, the Russian Empire was actually a collection of various ethnic groups stretching from Eastern Europe to the Yellow Sea in Asia. Lenin established the Bolshevik Central Committee in 1912, giving a new bureaucratic structure to the movement, and he named Stalin as the expert on racial minorities. It was with his rise in the Communist Party that Iosif Dzhugashvili adopted the name Joseph Stalin, a last name that means "steel" in Russian.

This vast empire was drawn into World War I in 1914. The czar called on his hungry, bitter masses to march to the front, poorly armed and poorly trained, to fight the German army. Despite their disgruntlement, the country bristled with soldiers; nearly 6 million Russians donned uniforms and marched toward miserable deaths at the front.

When World War I broke out, Stalin was in prison in Kureika in northern Russia near the Arctic Circle. He had been living as a fugitive since he started his revolutionary activities in Georgia. The czar's police had taken note of Stalin, and when he was captured shortly before the outbreak of war, he was sentenced to a four-year prison term. But before his sentence was completed, however, Stalin was called to active service. The Russian army had suffered many losses at the front, and the czar decided to draft men who had been exiled to the vast wastelands of Siberia.

When he reached the mobilization station, Stalin was rejected for military service because his left arm was longer than his right.

Russia in 1914

Thus, instead of going to the front, Stalin returned to his old revolutionary campaigning.

The Triumph of Revolution

Three years of war left Russia destitute. The middle classes turned on the czar after watching their sons march off to the frigid winter conditions of the front. Even the army turned against the czar. Faced with this mutiny, he was forced to abdicate. In his place, noncommunist opponents of the czar established a provisional government. The new government made peace with Germany, and Russian soldiers returned to the political chaos that had engulfed Russia. The Communists saw this as the chance to seize power. Leon Trotsky, a leader of the Mensheviks, exclaimed: "The streets of Petrograd again speak the language of 1905,"[33] referring to the date of a failed uprising against the czar. Stalin, suddenly free from threat of arrest by the czar's police, quickly returned to Petrograd to take over the editorship of the Bolshevik newspaper *Pravda* (*Truth*).

The political chaos that greeted Stalin on his arrival in Petrograd quickly escalated to outright revolution. On November 6, 1917, the Bolsheviks seized the Winter Palace and captured members of the provisional government. They established the Council of Peo-

Bolsheviks storm the Winter Palace in Petrograd during the revolution in 1917. The Bolsheviks replaced the provisional Russian government with a Communist regime.

ple's Commissars as the governing body, with Lenin as its leader. Lenin promised peace and prosperity to the Russian people.

Nevertheless, counterrevolutionary forces, who wanted to establish a liberal democracy or reinstate the czar, continued to fight the Communists throughout Russia. Revolution had turned into civil war. Stalin became Lenin's right-hand man and organized both political and military maneuvers in the war against the "White" Russians, as supporters of both the czar and the provisional government were called. One of his chief victories was the defense of Tsaritsyn, a major city on the lower Volga River, from an attack by White Russians. In 1928 Stalin renamed the city Stalingrad, in his own honor.

Struggle for Power

The Russian Revolution of 1917 transformed the world's largest country into a Communist state. By 1923, however, Lenin, the revolution's leader, was dying. While Lenin's health deteriorated, Stalin and the other Bolshevik leaders jockeyed for power. Stalin excelled at the game. His oafish appearance—with his pockmarked face, anti-intellectual attitude, and his love of violence—led others to underestimate him. "He's not an intellectual like the other people you will meet," wrote American journalist John Reed, who witnessed the 1917 Russian Revolution firsthand. "He's not even particularly well informed, but he knows what he wants. He's got will-power, and he's going to be on top of the pile some day."[34]

Leon Trotsky, leader of the Mensheviks and rival of Stalin.

Before his death, Lenin helped Stalin win election as the general secretary of the Communist Party. But Lenin soon regretted his support of Stalin and favored Leon Trotsky to take over leadership of the party after his death. Before Lenin died in January 1924, he had threatened to undo Stalin's work by writing an open testament that criticized the Georgian strongman. "Having become General Secretary," wrote Lenin, "[Stalin] has unlimited authority concentrated in his hands, and I am not sure whether he will be capable of using that authority with sufficient caution."[35]

Lenin (left) originally chose Stalin (right) as his successor but later withdrew his support, fearing that unlimited power in Stalin's hands would be dangerous.

One person who tried to moderate Stalin's ruthlessness at this time was his second wife, Nadezhda Alliluyeva. The couple had married in 1919 and had had two children: a son, Vasily, and a daughter, Svetlana. But Stalin's ambitions never lay in domestic happiness, and he devoted most of his attention to politics.

Upon Lenin's death, Stalin moved quickly to push Trotsky out of the way and to present himself as Lenin's legitimate successor. Stalin held a spectacular funeral for Lenin and presented himself prominently before the Russian mourners. "Comrades! We Communists are people of a special cast," Stalin pronounced jubilantly. "We are fashioned of special stuff. We are the ones who form the army of the great proletarian general, the army of Comrade Lenin."[36]

By the following year, Stalin had succeeded in squeezing Trotsky out of the ruling circle. Stalin eventually had him expelled from the Communist Party altogether and deported from Russia. Stalin's revenge was thorough and deadly. He had Trotsky pursued by assassins, who caught up with him in Mexico City in 1940 and murdered him with an ice pick.

Man of Steel

Stalin emerged from the struggle with Trotsky as the general secretary of the Communist Party and supreme leader of the Soviet

Union, as Russia was called by the Communists. Lenin had feared that Stalin would not wield power cautiously, and those fears proved well founded. Stalin abandoned Lenin's more cautious approach to economic policy and brought all agriculture, commerce, and industry under government control. Stalin laid out a Five-Year Plan for the collectivization of agriculture and other reforms. Peasants were forced off their land and onto giant collective farms. As many as 25 million rural farmers were forced into these state-owned projects.

Families were uprooted from their traditional way of life and their personal ambitions were cast aside in the name of the state. Those who resisted faced persecution by the secret police force known as the People's Commissariat of Internal Affairs, also known by its Russian initials, NKVD, and by the army. The kulaks, as these recalcitrant peasants were called, faced mass arrest and exile in Siberia or death by firing squad. Stalin's prison camps in Siberia, called gulags, had much tighter security than Stalin had known when he was a prisoner of the czar.

The prison camps were ringed by barbed wire and armed guards. Prisoners were forced to work for long hours chopping

Russians who resisted Stalin's reforms were sent to gulags, or prison camps. Millions of people died of disease or starvation in these camps.

firewood, farming, and doing other manual labor, and their meals were scant. Many kulaks starved to death. It is estimated that about 10 million peasants died either indirectly due to Stalin's land reforms or in the gulags.

Stalin boasted that the collective farms were a worker's paradise and were populated by what he called "the New Soviet Man"—a hardworking peasant who obeyed the supreme authority of Stalin. But the reality was very different. The collective farms were often poorly organized, and the earth was overfarmed, resulting in poor yields and eventually famine.

Although collectivized farming failed to produce the abundance of food that was promised, Stalin's industrial programs had more success. Communism's ideological father, Karl Marx, had taught that revolution was based on the industrial worker, and Stalin set the blast furnaces burning day and night to bring industrial progress to the Soviet Union. The cities blackened with the smoke of furnaces, and men and women worked side by side in the creation of a new industrial nation. Stalin had inherited a backward agrarian country, but through the blood and sweat of his people, he forged an industrial state—held up by steel and lubricated by oil.

Stalin held everyone accountable for meeting the goals that he set. When industrial managers failed to meet production quotas, Stalin arranged show trials in which those who fell short of expectations were forced to confess to crimes. "Show trials," wrote historian Martin Gilbert, "were a feature of Stalin's exercise of control; the public pointing the accusatory fingers, and absurd charges, prior to the inevitable conviction and severe sentences of imprisonment and long Siberian exile."[37] The less fortunate of the accused were shot.

Stalin claimed that these counterrevolutionaries harmed the Soviet economic system. If a talented industrial manager or scientist failed Stalin's expectations, he or she was executed or imprisoned without regard to past accomplishments. These purges robbed the country of some of its greatest scientific and managerial talent.

Stalin's ruthlessness in the achievement of his national goals was heightened by his lust for blood and by his paranoia. Seemingly without reason, he accused even his closest supporters of counterrevolutionary activities. Stalin murdered almost all of the early members of the Communist Central Committee, fearing that they would challenge his authority. Even the NKVD, Stalin's secret police force that carried out his orders, came under suspicion. These henchmen, despite their loyalty, soon suffered the same fate that they had been meting out to victims around the country.

Even Stalin's family was shattered by his cruelty. His wife committed suicide in 1932, and his son, Vasily, after being promoted in the Soviet air force, died from alcoholism. Later, his favorite child, Svetlana, would flee the Soviet Union after Stalin's death and write harshly of her father from abroad.

Other Soviet citizens fared just as badly. In terms of human life, Stalin's policies were extremely costly to the Soviet Union. Perhaps 20 million Soviets died either by Stalin's direct orders or as a result of his attempts to restructure his nation's economy. Death on an even greater scale awaited, however, as one of Stalin's fellow dictators, Adolf Hitler, readied Germany for war.

In order to stay in power, Stalin executed his opposition and even his close associates.

Breaker of Nations

As Hitler prepared for World War II, he devised a plan to keep the Soviet Union out of the war until his forces were strong enough to meet the Russians in battle. In 1939 Stalin signed a treaty of nonaggression offered by Hitler. Under secret terms of this pact, the two ideological enemies agreed that Poland would be divided between them. Germany would take the western portion, and the Soviet Union would take the eastern. This cynical pact between the mortal enemies was soon called "the Pact of Blood."

Stalin knew that Hitler would not long honor the treaty and that Russia would one day face German aggression. As soon as Stalin signed the pact, he began fortifying his western border and building up the Soviet military. The treaty, Stalin calculated, had bought time for the Russians to prepare for war.

As Stalin expected, his treacherous ally finally broke his promise and invaded the Soviet Union in June 1941. Despite Stalin's foresight, Russian defenses proved inadequate. The Nazi blitzkrieg thrust deep into Soviet territory. Acting as commander in chief of the armed forces, Stalin directed the Soviet war effort himself.

When the German army reached Moscow, the Soviet capital, Stalin prepared its defense. German soldiers reached the suburbs of the capital. Stalin's willpower and his readiness to sacrifice his own soldiers in great battles allowed the Soviets to mount fierce resistance to the German onslaught. Through repeated bloody counterattacks, the Russians finally forced the Germans to withdraw from Moscow.

The successful defense of the capital boosted morale among the Russian soldiers, but the greatest test for the Soviet forces came at Stalingrad, which the Germans besieged in September 1942. Stalin, as usual, ordered his troops to fight to their deaths. In street-by-street fighting, the Soviet soldiers did just that. The casualties reached staggering numbers as the battle dragged into the frigid winter months. Stalin eventually got reinforcements to the besieged city, and the Russians captured ninety thousand German soldiers.

The Battle of Stalingrad signaled a turning point in the war. German forces, extended far beyond their supply lines from Germany, ground to a halt. This city on the Volga River marked the deepest point of the German advance into Russian territory. The vastness of the Soviet Union and the subzero temperatures of its winters proved too much for the German war machine.

Stalin terrorized his generals into a counteroffensive. Under threat of death, they responded with brutal attacks on the German army. Stalin made his generals' task easier by declaring that all Soviet soldiers who surrendered would be considered traitors. A British military officer witnessed the fear even in Stalin's top military personnel during a wartime visit to the Soviet Union: "He moved stealthily like a wild animal in search of prey, and his eyes were shrewd and full of cunning. He never looked one in the face. But he had a great dignity and his personality was dominating. As he entered the room, every Russian froze into silence showing all too plainly the constant fear in which they lived."[38]

The Red Army had little choice but to fight to the death, and nobody was spared in the defense of Russia. When his own son, Yakov, was captured by the Germans, Stalin called him a

Stalin's eldest son, Yakov, was captured by the Germans, but the Soviet dictator refused to negotiate for his release.

(Left to right) Stalin, Franklin D. Roosevelt, and Winston Churchill at the Tehran Conference in 1943. That he was included in talks about how postwar Europe would be run greatly enhanced Stalin's prestige.

traitor and a coward. And when the Germans offered to release Yakov in a prisoner exchange, Stalin refused. "In the Red Army," Stalin quipped, "it takes more courage to retreat than to advance."[39]

World War II proved to be an enormous boon for Stalin's international prestige. The Soviet leader was included in the major conferences with British prime minister Winston Churchill and American president Franklin Delano Roosevelt. As the war neared its end, the "Big Three" Allied leaders agreed that the Russians would be the first to enter Berlin. Stalin was awarded this prize out of respect for the millions of Soviets who had died fighting the Germans.

The Cold Warrior

After the war, the unnatural alliance between the Communist Soviet Union and the democracies of Great Britain and the United States deteriorated. Stalin made it clear that his liberation of Eastern Europe was actually a new conquest. "This war is unlike all past wars," he said. "Whoever occupies a territory imposes his own social system. Everyone imposes his system as far as his army can advance."[40]

In 1946 Britain's prime minister commented on the long-term implications of Stalin's actions:

> From Settin in the Baltic to Trieste in the Adriatic, an iron curtain has descended across the continent. Behind that line lie all the capitals of the ancient states of Central Europe . . . and all are subject in one form or another, not only to Soviet influence but to a very high and, in many cases, increasing measure of control from Moscow.[41]

Stalin waged a new kind of war with the liberal democracies of Western Europe and the United States: a Cold War fought with threats and marked by suspicion and fear. Soviet troops enforced Stalin's wishes across a broad swath of Eastern Europe.

Domestic Terror

At home, Stalin renewed his purges of anyone he thought might oppose him. He seized Jewish doctors, political enemies, and uncooperative workers. The Trans-Siberian Railway, laden with these unfortunates, puffed across the melancholy steppes of Russia toward the gulags, where starvation and death waited.

Stalin's reign of terror ended on March 5, 1953, when he died suddenly. In the twenty-five years of his leadership of the Soviet Union's Communist Party, Stalin had killed more of his own people than had any national leader in history. Succeeding generations of Russians would remember Stalin more for his brutality than for his accomplishments. He had transformed the Soviet Union from a feudal agrarian society into a modern industrialized nation. But his reign of terror permanently colored his reputation.

In October 1961 the USSR's Twenty-second Party Congress ordered the removal of Stalin's embalmed body from a place of honor in Red Square. It was reburied in a plain grave beside the Kremlin wall. And the city of Stalingrad was renamed Volgograd, after the Volga River which enriches the region.

CHAPTER 5

Mao Zedong

The success of the Communist revolution in the Soviet Union boosted the ambitions of Communists all over the world. One country that had long suffered under weakened dynastic rule like that of the Russian czars was China. And in 1949 a former peasant named Mao Zedong, triumphant in his own revolution, proclaimed the Communist People's Republic of China.

The Rebellious Son of a Rich Peasant

Mao Zedong was born on December 26, 1893, in the village of Shaoshan in the southern Chinese province of Hunan. Hunan, which receives generous rains from the monsoons that sweep across southern China annually, is one of the main rice-growing regions of China.

Mao's father, Mao Xunsheng, like other peasants, harvested rice and kept pigs. Unlike many other peasants, however, Mao Xunsheng prospered. What goods the family did not use Mao Xunsheng sold at market. From the profits, he earned enough to enlarge the family lands and to lend money to others, which earned him still more money.

On Mao Zedong, as the eldest of four children, fell the heavy responsibilities of a Chinese son. Starting at the age of five, Mao worked knee-deep in the muddy waters of the rice paddies helping his father bring in the crop. Mao's father was stern, sometimes despotic, and Mao felt closer to his mother, who often mediated disputes between father and son.

Mao Zedong was born into a prosperous peasant family in the village Shaoshan, in Hunan province.

Mao Xunsheng wanted an easier life for his son. For peasants, one hope for escape was a government job, but such jobs only went to those who scored well on state exams. At this time, Mao Zedong was studying with a tutor, who taught him geography, history, calligraphy, and, most importantly, the Confucian classics; mastery of the Confucian classics was essential if a student was to pass the state exams.

Mao proved to be a gifted scholar, and he often quoted Confucius in arguments with his father. "Accused of laziness by his father," wrote Mao biographer Peter Carter, "he quoted Confucius, saying that the father's role was to be kind and caring. Accused of rebellion he quoted again, answering that the father being bigger, ought to work harder than the children."[42] These small acts of rebellion included the spurning of a marriage arranged by his father. Arranged marriages were common in China, and children were seldom consulted about or involved in the decision-making process. When Mao was fourteen, he was married to a local girl. Mao refused to live with the girl and never considered her his wife.

Mao believed that his future lay in the great world outside his village and read constantly as an escape from village life. Though

Confucius, a sixth-century B.C. philosopher, promoted a code of behavior that stressed learning and a respect for authority.

Mao was mastering the Confucian classics, he preferred the historical romances of Chinese literature: *The Outlaws of the Marsh*, *Journey to the West*, and *The Romance of the Three Kingdoms*. These are tales of rebellion and adventure, full of colorful episodes, banditry, and triumphs of the weak over the strong and the just over the wicked.

The End of Empire

In the spring of 1910, severe drought caused famine in Hunan. Rebellions smoldered in the region as peasants rioted against tax collectors and looted food stores. Mao's family, now mildly prosperous, weathered the famine better than most. During his winter break from school, Mao was sent around to collect debts for his father, which he did. On the road, however, he met some hungry peasants and gave them his father's money.

It was not long after this minor act of rebellion that Mao, hungry for a wider view of the world, traveled to the provincial capital of Changsha to further his studies. Changsha bubbled with talk of insurrection and bristled with armed men. Mao witnessed brutal executions in which imperial officials cleaved off the heads of rebels who fought to overthrow the emperor and establish a republic headed by an elected leader.

This rebel movement was led by the charismatic Sun Yat-sen, whose writings could be found in Changsha and throughout China. Mao, studying in Changsha, read not only the works of Chinese reformers like Sun Yat-sen but also biographies of Western leaders such as George Washington, Napoléon, the duke of Wellington, and British prime minister William Gladstone. And in the provincial capital, Mao witnessed history being made as China changed before his eyes.

In 1911 the Republicans rose against the emperor after a group of the emperor's opponents accidentally set off an explosion in the busy trading city of Wuhan in the Hubei province, just to the north of Hunan. Rebellion spread quickly across southern China, where Republicans clashed with imperial troops.

The eighteen-year-old Mao, caught up in the revolutionary fervor, cut his long braid of hair, known as a queue—a symbol of the ruling dynasty—and donned the Western-style uniform of the swaggering Republican troops. By doing so, Mao branded himself an outlaw, pitched against the emperor and all the might of the imperial armies. By early 1912 the Republicans had triumphed, ending more than two thousand years of imperial rule.

"The uprising," write historians Jonathan D. Spence and Ann-ping Chin, "was a formative military experience: a first encounter with violence, ideology and politics. This was the case with the young Mao Zedong."[43]

The Political Education of Mao Zedong

Headed by Sun Yat-sen, the Republicans moved the capital of China from Beijing (which means "Northern Capital" in Chinese) to the city of Nanjing ("Southern Capital") on the Yangtze River in central China. The establishment of a republic, with elected officials for the more than 500 million people of China, was an experiment on a grand scale.

In addition to completely changing how China was governed, other aspects of life changed as well. Educational reforms were instituted, and the ancient practice of foot binding, which left a woman crippled for life, was outlawed. Mao agreed with Sun's revolutionary views on women, and his second wife, Yang Kaihui, the daughter of one of Mao's teachers in Changsha, shared her husband's revolutionary outlook. But the most profound Western influence on China in the twentieth century was to be Communism. Mao had traveled to Beijing some months earlier and, working as a librarian at Peking University, he read the works of Karl Marx and the works of Lenin.

With the editors of *New Youth*, a radical periodical he wrote for in Beijing, Mao traveled to Shanghai. It was there that he helped found the Chinese Communist Party in 1921. Although he modeled the party on Russia's Communist Party, Mao, even at this early stage, was convinced that the power of Chinese society lay in the peasants rather than the industrial workers. In spite of this unorthodox view, the popularity of the Communist Party grew among students and industrial workers in China's cities.

As the Communists gained strength across China, Sun Yat-sen, at the head of the government, tried to unify China, which had become a collection of warring factions led by individual warlords. Sun managed to hold together an alliance with the Communists, but the warlords continued fighting among themselves.

Sun would never see his dream of a single unified republic in China. Sun's death in 1925 set off a scramble for control of the ruling party, the Kuomintang. Chiang Kai-shek, a young militarist who had headed the Nationalists' Whampoa Military Academy, emerged as the party leader. Chiang had a visceral dislike for Communists. Moreover, he was backed by the rich: aristocratic landlords, bankers, and merchants. It would not be long before his party and the Communist Party would come to blows.

For a time, Chiang upheld the alliance with the Communists, but in 1927 Chiang moved against the Communists in Shanghai. The city was at that time a hotbed of all sorts of illegal activity and political intrigue. The Communists harangued the citizenry, trying to win them over to their point of view, and criminal organizations such as the Green Gangs controlled the lucrative opium trade and the numerous brothels visited by the Shanghainese and by the Western residents of the international quarters of the city.

Chiang found his allies among these criminal organizations. At dawn on April 27, the Green Gangs, at the direction of Chiang, stormed the offices of Shanghai labor unions and other Communist gathering spots, beating Communists and smashing their headquarters. Kuomintang agents mingled in the street fighting and executed Communists whenever they could capture them.

Mao avoided the violence in Shanghai because he was working for the Communist Party in Hunan to organize the peasants. Nevertheless, Chiang ordered Mao's arrest; he was captured later that year. Mao escaped from his captors. His second wife, Yang Kaihui, was not so fortunate and was captured by Chiang's forces in 1930 and was executed. The treachery of Chiang Kai-shek and the personal loss of his wife in the political fight hardened Mao's

Mao, shown here speaking to a group of peasants, helped form the Chinese Communist Party in 1921 and contributed to the growth of its popularity.

Chiang Kai-shek, head of the Kuomintang, despised Communism and quickly entered into battle with Mao Zedong.

resolve to win control of China for the Communists, and they began to organize their forces. The stage was set for an all-out battle between the Nationalists under Chiang Kai-shek and the Communists led by Mao Zedong.

Civil War

Mao and Zhu De, the commander of the Red Army, as the Communist forces were called, withdrew to the south to prepare to fight the Nationalists, who still vastly outnumbered them. This was the beginning of the Chinese Civil War, which would last nearly two decades.

Mao strongly felt that the fight with Chiang Kai-shek would be critical. "Chiang Kai-shek," wrote Mao, "always tries to wrest every ounce of power and every ounce of gain from the people. And we? Our policy is to give him tit for tat and to fight for every inch of land. As Chiang Kai-shek is now sharpening his swords, we must sharpen ours too."[44]

Knowing that the Communists were not ready to face Chiang's forces in pitched battles, Mao adopted the military strategy of guerrilla warfare, summed up by Zhu De:

> When the enemy advances, we retreat.
> When the enemy halts and encamps, we harass them.
> When the enemy seeks to avoid battle, we attack.
> When the enemy retreats, we pursue.[45]

On the political front, Mao proved to be a masterful propagandist, drawing many supporters to the Communist cause through his speeches, writings, and his fair treatment of the people that he encountered while marching with the Red Army. Mao's order to the Red Army to pay for whatever they ate when they passed through villages and to treat villagers with respect, won many converts to the Communist side, even though many of the new adherents had little understanding of Communism itself.

In the southern province of Jiangxi, Mao had set up a Chinese Soviet republic from which the Red Army could launch attacks against the Nationalists. In 1934 Chiang's troops marched on Jiangxi, forcing a complete evacuation of the Communists. The retreat that followed turned into an epic journey over some eight thousand miles.

The Long March, as the journey was later called, took the Communists west and then north through rugged Chinese countryside

The Long March

and lasted for a year. Finally the Red Army encamped at a remote cave complex in the village of Yan'an in Shaanxi province. It was here at Yan'an that Mao met Jiang Qing, an actress from Shanghai. A fervent Communist, Jiang Qing also became one of Mao's most ardent supporters, and the couple later married.

World War

For his courage and leadership during the Long March, Mao, at age forty-three, was elected to the post of chairman of the Chinese Communist Party, the highest office in the party. From their base at Yan'an, the Communists regrouped, then restarted their guerrilla campaign against the Nationalists and against a new combatant in northern China: the Japanese.

The Japanese, as the first stage of a grand military plan for the conquest of east Asia, had invaded an area of northern China called Manchuria in 1931 and by 1937 were moving southward along the coast. As they moved from one city to the next, the Japanese treated the Chinese harshly. They killed unarmed men, raped women, and stole and destroyed property. Despite Japanese ruthlessness, Chiang adopted a policy of appeasement toward the Japanese despite their ferocious and destructive advance through China, and he chose instead to pursue the Red Army in the belief that Mao and the other Communists were the real threat to China. "The Japanese," he said, "are a disease of the skin. The communists are a disease of the heart."[46]

Mao, on the other hand, believed that the Japanese must be defeated at all costs and offered to ally his forces with Chiang's to fight the Japanese. Mao got his way after the spectacular kidnapping of Chiang Kai-shek by a warlord in the northern city of Xi'an in 1936. In what became known as the Xi'an Incident, the warlord, Zhang Xueliang, lured Chiang to Xi'an, kidnapped him, and threatened to kill him unless he agreed to form a united front with the Communists. Zhang, who had originally been allied with Chiang, had been driven out of Manchuria by the Japanese; he hated the foreign invaders so much that he turned against Chiang in order to forge this united front, an arrangement which lasted until 1945, when Japan was defeated.

The alliance between Mao and Chiang broke down frequently, and directly after the war the two turned on each other again. The Red Army swelled as the Nationalist forces withered. Peasants scoffed at the arrogance of Nationalist soldiers and their corrupt generals, and they refused to come to their aid. Chiang's policy of conscripting peasants into his army when he passed through their villages only pushed more rural Chinese into the ranks of the Communist army.

The overwhelming support Mao had garnered in the country-side bore fruit in the last phase of the civil war. In 1949 Chiang withdrew in defeat to the island of Taiwan, where he claimed to lead the Republic of China. On October 1, 1949, Mao proclaimed the founding of the People's Republic of China from the Gate of Heavenly Peace in Beijing, which he made, once again, the Chinese capital. "China," said Mao, "has stood up."[47]

The Great Helmsman

The civil war caused great suffering in China, and Mao inherited a ruined country. Industry, agriculture, and trade had been all but destroyed, and famine racked the country. But Mao saw in the chaos an opportunity to create a new society. The peasants—the great swarming masses—had found a voice for the first time in Chinese history. And most importantly, China had finally thrown

Japanese forces enter China. Destructive as the invading Japanese army was, Chiang believed that the Communists were a greater threat to China.

Mao speaks with peasants. During the civil war in China, most peasants supported Mao and the Communists.

off the yoke of foreign occupation: The Japanese had been driven out in defeat, and the European imperial powers had withdrawn as well.

While the Red Army, renamed the People's Liberation Army, marched throughout China, routing the last pockets of resistance, Mao devised experimental projects to bring China into the modern world. He collectivized landholdings, winning the affection of the peasants and the ire of the landlords. Farms were henceforth owned by the state and worked by large production brigades. Workers ate together in communal halls and often slept in dormitories.

In 1949 Mao visited Russia, where he wrested from Joseph Stalin pledges of financial and technical support. The two signed a thirty-year pact agreeing to friendship, alliance, and mutual aid. Stalin warned Mao against moving too quickly with land-reform projects.

Stalin viewed Mao as a threat to his leadership of international Communism. Mao, in return, was wary of Stalin and Russian advisers. "They did not allow China to make revolution," Mao said. "This was in 1945, when Stalin tried to prevent the Chinese revolution by saying that we must collaborate with Chiang Kai-shek. Otherwise the Chinese nation would perish. At that time, we did not carry this into effect, and the revolution was victorious."[48]

Non-communist countries, unaware of these Chinese-Soviet rifts, shivered at the thought of so much of the globe in the grip of

Communism. The United States, which emerged from World War II as a military and economic superpower, took up the crusade against "the Reds." Hostility between the United States and the Soviet Union simmered during a period known as the Cold War as each jockeyed for greater influence around the world.

Despite his rivalry with Stalin, Mao saw the United States as the greatest threat to his newly proclaimed nation. The U.S. government had recognized the Republic of China (Taiwan) as the legitimate Chinese government and poured money and weapons into the island. Mao saw the presence of American military bases, the result of the Allied victory over Japan in World War II, as a ring of imperialism encircling China.

Relations between the United States and China flashed into a shooting war on the Korean peninsula when Chinese troops clashed with United Nations forces just south of the Yalu River, which forms the border between China and North Korea. The Korean War (1951–1953) was the first real test of Mao's ability to defend Chinese sovereignty. The Korean War was costly for Mao.

A bomb destroys a warehouse during the Korean War. The conflict between North Korea, backed by China, and South Korea, aided by the United Nations, proved costly to Mao, both personally and politically.

He lost a son, and some Communist Party officials criticized Mao for involving China in the conflict. But Mao could claim that China had successfully defended its border, and support for the country's Communist leadership swelled as a result.

The Communist Party was the sole ruling organ of the Chinese state, and Mao as party chairman enjoyed power as absolute as that which China's emperors had wielded. Mao's will was enforced by the might of the People's Liberation Army, but still Mao feared that the concentration of power would cause Communist Party officials to lose their revolutionary fervor and slide into stale bureaucracy.

A Hundred Flowers Bloom

To prevent the Chinese Communist Party from slipping away from the people, Mao initiated the Hundred Flowers Campaign in 1957. The campaign invited criticism of the government and opened debate on the future of the arts in China. "Letting a hundred flowers blossom and a hundred schools of thought contend," wrote Mao, "is the policy for promoting the progress of the arts and the sciences and a flourishing socialist culture in our land."[49]

To Mao's surprise, criticism poured forth from intellectuals and students. They criticized the government's handling of education, restrictions on free speech, and the easy life of the high Communist Party members, whose positions of influence isolated them from the people they ruled.

With the critics lured into the open by Mao's promises of free and open debate, the trap slammed shut. Mao labeled the critics "rightists" and "reactionaries" and sent many of them to work in the countryside. The antirightist campaign that followed lasted for three years and purged many of Mao's leading critics from power.

The legacy of the Hundred Flowers Campaign was fear. Afterward, critics of the government kept their opinions to themselves or expressed them cautiously, avoiding the spotlight and the punishment of the government. Now a curtain of fear descended between the Chinese and their government.

In the society that Mao's policies fostered, the individual was to ignore his individuality and think only as a part of the group, part of the state. Even artistic expression—which the Hundred Flowers Campaign promised to encourage—would now serve only the national spirit. "All our literature and art," wrote Mao, "are for the masses of the people. . . . They are created for the workers, peasants and soldiers and are for their use."[50]

The Great Leap Forward

Mao redirected individual ambitions into a national effort toward industrial and agricultural development. The Great Leap Forward, as he called this new campaign, intensified production in the countryside. On collective farms, peasants tried new agricultural methods to increase production. Technical schools were also established in the countryside to teach rural workers to produce basic industrial goods.

Primitive furnaces popped up across the country, and ore was smelted into iron and steel. The output of these so-called backyard furnaces, however, was of such low quality as to be useless. Even the original agricultural advances withered as the soil was overfarmed. It soon became clear that Mao's ideological energy outstripped reality. The Great Leap Forward fell short, resulting in a famine that cost as many as 20 million lives.

Despite the agricultural failure of the Great Leap Forward, China was making technological progress. Arms manufacturing, for example, increased dramatically. In 1964 China exploded its first atomic bomb, bringing the nation into the exclusive "nuclear club." Mao's radical Communist ideology made the leaders of many nations uneasy, as did his cavalier attitude toward nuclear weapons. "The atomic bomb," he said, "is a paper tiger used by U.S. reactionaries to scare people. It looks terrible, but in fact it isn't."[51]

Mao Unleashes Chaos

Members of the Communist Party hierarchy also criticized Mao for the failure of the Great Leap Forward. Their concern was for the stability and preservation of the party. Mao once again accused his critics of rightist sympathies. To counter party criticism, Mao unleashed the Great Proletarian Cultural Revolution in 1966. Mao's wife, Jiang Qing, spearheaded the movement among students and scholars, who organized rallies at universities and openly criticized government officials.

Mao's wife Jiang Qing led the Cultural Revolution, which Mao started as a means of eliminating critics in the Communist Party.

Soon China was awash with chanting students publicly berating the older generation for going soft. Students formed "Red Guard" detachments and adopted paramilitary dress: blue "Mao" suits, workers caps, and red armbands. They were armed with the quotations from Chairman Mao, which had been collected and published in a pocket-size edition with red covers.

The students chanted the revolutionary aphorisms from Mao's book of quotations in massive gatherings in public squares. The largest rallies were held in Tiananmen Square in front of the Communist Party headquarters in Beijing. In villages around the country, those accused of harboring feelings against the Communist Party had their heads shaved in public spectacles designed to humiliate citizens who lacked revolutionary fervor.

The Red Guards also seized on Mao's dislike of religion. Taoists, Buddhists, and Christians, whose creeds had been under attack since the founding of the People's Republic of China, were beaten by the Red Guards, who also desecrated their places of

The Red Guard was made up of students, like those pictured here, devoted to Mao and revolutionary ideals.

In 1972, Richard Nixon became the first American president to visit Communist China and meet with Mao.

worship. Red Guards even smashed Confucian temples and vandalized the grave of Confucius in their frenzy.

By the following year Red Guard units were turning against each other. Anyone accused of any lack of revolutionary fervor was presumed to be guilty. China was descending into chaos. Mao knew that the Red Guards were making him a living god, and he feared for China's fate once he was dead. His picture hung in public squares, schools, offices, and homes throughout the country. "He was divine," wrote one Red Guard, "and the revolutionary tides rose and fell at his command."[52]

Mao Softens the Party Line

The Red Guards, with their fanatical belief in Mao, caused agriculture and industry to grind nearly to a halt in China. The nation became increasingly isolated. Sensing catastrophe, Mao disbanded the Red Guards and sent them to the countryside to vent their energy working the fields. The Cultural Revolution continued into the mid-1970s, but Mao had controlled the worst excesses of the Red Guards.

Others in China saw the need to end the country's isolation. Premier Zhou Enlai, one of Mao's comrades from the Long March, had helped convince Mao to dampen the zeal of the Red Guards and wanted China to restore diplomatic relations with the United States, which had been broken in 1949. Chairman Mao, at age seventy-nine, had also grown weary of isolation and agreed to a diplomatic exchange. Zhou first organized the table tennis matches between China and the United States. This "Ping-Pong diplomacy" led to more substantial talks with the Americans. The following year, Richard Nixon became the first American president to visit the People's Republic of China.

The sometimes awkward meeting between the American president and Mao proved to be a success for both leaders. Mao's meeting with Nixon quelled Americans' fears about China. China had once again begun to look outward. But Mao was an old man, and on September 9, 1976, Mao Zedong, founder of the world's most populous Communist state, died. His body was preserved in twenty-two liters of formaldehyde and was displayed in a mausoleum on Tiananmen Square.

In the years after Mao's death, moderates in the Communist Party gained control. More radical members like Mao's wife, Jiang Qing, and other comrades were given long prison terms for their roles in creating the worst excesses of the Cultural Revolution.

The future of many of Mao's policies is in doubt. Following Mao's death, Deng Xiaoping emerged as the new Chinese leader. Deng abandoned Mao's Marxist economics, and he guided China toward a path of greater economic prosperity by opening the country to limited capitalism. Deng's pragmatism is captured by one of his favorite sayings: "It doesn't matter whether the cat is black or white as long as it catches the mouse."[53]

CHAPTER 6

Fidel Castro

The fall of China, as the Americans called Mao's victory in 1949, heightened fears in the West of the spread of Communism. Not only was the Soviet Union—the world's largest country—Communist, but suddenly so, too, was China—the world's most populous nation.

The United States, the chief opponent of the Soviet Union throughout the Cold War, had long protected its own hemisphere from the spread of what it saw as "the Red Menace." But the 1958 overthrow of the U.S.-backed dictator Fulgencio Batista y Zaldívar in Cuba in a revolution led by Fidel Castro brought Communism into America's own backyard when Castro founded the first Communist state in the Western Hemisphere. As Castro moved to embrace Communism, the United States portrayed him as a potent threat to U.S. national security. The conflict between the Cuban dictator and the United States thrust Cuba onto the international scene, where it played a role greatly disproportionate to its size.

On the Plantation

From Castro's perspective, the Americans had inherited the mantle of imperialism from the Spanish, who had colonized Cuba centuries earlier. Though Cuba had gained its independence from Spain in 1901, the Cuban constitution permitted the United States to send troops into the island at will. The Americans' primary concern in the island was sugarcane, which was Cuba's main crop and was sold to the United States at a cheap price.

One of those sugarcane farmers was the father of Fidel Castro Ruz,

Fidel Castro established the first Communist state in the Western Hemisphere.

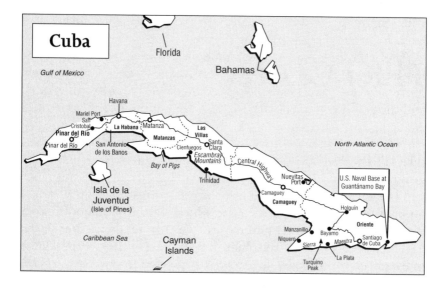

who was born on August 13, 1926. Fidel grew up on his father's sugarcane plantation in the Biran district, located in eastern Cuba. Fidel's father, Angel Castro, had emigrated from Spain and worked on the railways of the American-owned United Fruit Company. The United Fruit Company was just one of the many prosperous ventures owned by Americans but worked by Cuban laborers.

From working for the Americans, Angel Castro saved enough to start his own plantation, and by the time Fidel was born, Angel was a moderately wealthy man. After the death of his first wife, with whom he had two children, Angel Castro had five more children with his native Cuban cook, Lina Ruz Gonzalez. It was Lina who was the mother of Fidel.

Castro grew up on the plantation surrounded by laborers, merchants, and the expansive United Fruit Company, which owned land all around his father's estate. A deep resentment toward the Americans permeated Cuban society, and Fidel developed a sympathy with the plantation laborers and an aversion, like so many other Cubans, to the American plantation owners.

The Romance of Revolution

Fidel's parents sent him to school in Santiago de Cuba, a major city on the southeastern coast of the country, and then to Belen College, a Catholic high school in the Cuban capital, Havana, where his love of talking and his sympathy for the hard life of the plantation laborers led him into left-wing student politics. The young Castro, active and outgoing, became increasingly popular as a student leader and one of the chief orators on campus. His voice could be heard denouncing corrupt government officials and what he called American imperialism.

After graduation, Castro entered law school at the University of Havana in 1945 with an eye on a political career. The prestigious university had given Cuban society many of its political leaders, and the campus buzzed with the talk among politically active students. Castro, never one to stay out of an argument, soon became embroiled in the heated disputes among students over Cuba's future. The university had become a hotbed of opposition to the government, and opposition politicians wooed the student body.

"The university," writes historian Theodore Draper, "was less an institution of learning or a professional training school than a nursery of hothouse revolutionaries." Castro, Draper writes, "was early tempted to get his more meaningful and exciting experiences in extra-school political adventures."[54]

One of these political adventures was the failed invasion of the Dominican Republic. Cuba, at that time, harbored political dissidents from the Dominican Republic, where Generalissimo Rafael Trujillo Molina ruled with an iron fist. Castro and many other young leftists supported the Dominican insurgents, seeing their opposition to Trujillo as similar to the Cuban leftist opposition to Batista. In 1947 Castro joined with the Dominican exiles and other Cubans to launch an invasion of the Dominican Republic with the goal of overthrowing Trujillo. But Batista's agents, who infiltrated the student radicals and kept a close watch on their activities, were also watching Castro. The authorities got wind of the planned invasion and put an end to the project.

Castro, who had already been noted as a political dissident by the government, continued his political activities. The following year Castro attended a congress of Latin American students in Bogotá, Colombia. The gathering was a chance for Castro to meet other left-leaning students from Latin America and to boost his own stature as an opposition figure.

In 1947, Castro plotted with exiles from the Dominican Republic against their ruler, Generalissimo Rafael Trujillo (pictured).

The conference was fraught with political tensions, and during the proceedings the leader of the Colombian Liberal Party, Jorge Eliécer Gaitán, was assassinated. Gaitán was an extremely popular opposition leader, and his death sparked violence in the Colombian capital. The students joined the fighting in the streets. Castro, like other students, was outraged by the assassination. The young Cuban got hold of a rifle and a policeman's uniform and battled the police. After forty-eight hours of street fighting, Castro retreated to the Cuban embassy and then flew back to Cuba with the other students. The episode appears to have been something of a watershed in Castro's experience. "The spectacle of an absolutely spontaneous popular revolution," Castro later said, "has to have exercised a great influence on me."[55]

Castro resumed his law studies, but he carried on with his political work. The charismatic young leader had a growing following among his fellow students. One of his admirers was Mirta Diaz-Balart, a student in the philosophy department. Diaz-Balart's father and brother Rafel were government officials, and they strongly disapproved of Castro because of his antigovernment sentiments. But in 1948 the couple married in a Catholic church in eastern Cuba and then flew to Miami, Florida, for their honeymoon. The following year Diaz-Balart gave birth to a son, whom they named Fidelito ("little Fidel").

Opposition Politics

Castro emerged from law school with a family and a promising career in politics. He became a member of the Cuban People's Party, or Ortodoxos, which sought to reform Cuba's government, and he opened a small law practice representing members of the political opposition. His real passion was still in politics, and he longed to throw himself into the fray not as a lawyer but as a leader.

Castro looked on his student radicalism as a badge of honor and in later years took pride in his unflinching opposition to the government. "In an era of unprecedented corruption," he wrote, "when many youthful leaders had access to dozens of government positions and so many were corrupted, to have led student protests against that regime for several years, without ever having appeared on a government payroll, is worthy of some merit."[56]

But the government payrolls were Castro's next step, or so he thought. He ran for a seat in the House of Representatives as the Ortodoxos' candidate for the Havana district. Castro looked forward to haranguing government officials from a seat in the legislative body of Cuba.

Three months before the elections, however, former president Fulgencio Batista y Zaldívar overthrew the government of Carlos Prio Socarras. Batista claimed that his coup, staged in March 1954, was necessary to rid the government of corruption. In fact, his politics were heavily influenced by Fascism, and subsequent events suggest that Batista's regime was just as corrupt as his predecessor's had been.

Castro reacted to the coup with furious indignation and quickly joined the underground opposition movement with the aim of overthrowing Batista. The time for working with those he opposed was over. "The present moment," he wrote, "is revolutionary, not political. . . . The Revolution opens the way for true merit, for those who bare their chest and take up the standard. A Revolutionary Party needs young revolutionary leadership drawn from the people in whose hands Cuba can be saved."[57]

Fulgencio Batista (pictured) served as president of Cuba from 1940 to 1944, and seized power again in 1954 when he overthrew Carlos Prio Socarras.

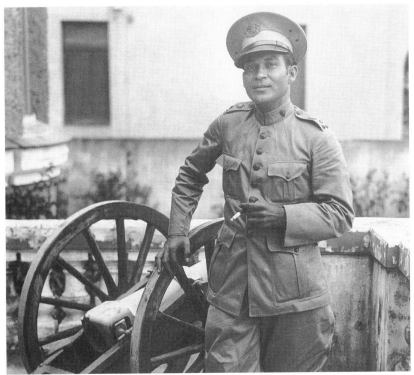

Suicide Raid

Castro's revolutionary action came in the form of a suicidal assault on the Moncada army post in Santiago de Cuba. On July 26, 1953, Castro led a party of 160 fellow revolutionaries armed with weapons they had scraped up the money to buy. As the revolutionaries advanced, however, they stumbled upon an army patrol, which alerted the entire garrison. With the element of surprise lost, the assault was quickly turned back by withering fire from fortified positions.

Three of Castro's men were killed outright. Sixty-eight were captured, tortured, and then executed in the aftermath of the Moncada disaster. Castro and his brother Raul also were captured and awaited almost certain death in prison. The assault on Moncada was a military disaster that cost the lives of half of his men, but the assault and Castro's subsequent trial proved to be a propaganda victory. The brutality of Batista's regime was underscored, and Castro gained national fame and popular sympathy, even as he shuffled off to prison in irons.

While Castro served nineteen months of his fifteen-year prison sentence on the Isle of Pines, his popularity grew throughout Cuba. New supporters agitated for his release, and Batista finally commuted the sentences of Castro, his brother Raul, and the other revolutionaries.

The speech that Castro had made at his trial, titled "History Will Absolve Me," had been widely reprinted, and the Moncada assault gained its place in the revolutionary lore of Cuba. Though it had been a military failure, the raid had won the hearts of many Cubans. Castro was earning his place among the pantheon of revolutionaries who had fought against brutal dictators earlier in the history of the island. The popular support for the jailed insurgents only heightened Castro's belief that a revolution against the Batista regime could succeed.

Preparing for the Final Blow

After his release, Castro found himself being closely watched by the nervous dictator. Fearing that he might again be arrested, Castro traveled to Mexico, choosing to continue the crusade against Batista's regime from abroad. Castro recruited Cuban exiles for his movement, which he named the 26th of July Movement after the date of the Moncada assault.

With the help of his brother Raul and Ernesto "Che" Guevara, a young Argentine doctor who had been active in other revolutionary movements, Castro secured arms and financial support for an inva-

Che Guevara (pictured), an Argentine physician who had experience in other revolutionary movements, joined forces with Castro to end Batista's regime.

sion force. They trained in steamy conditions, marching through swamps, practicing with their rifles, and living off sparse rations. While Castro traveled to the United States to raise money for the expedition, Che Guevara kindled the revolutionary spirit of the Fidelistas with his tales of revolution in other parts of Latin America.

Castro's efforts were in some ways actually aided by Batista and his cronies. As historian Arthur Schlesinger Jr. writes,

> The character of the Batista regime in Cuba made a violent popular reaction almost inevitable. The rapacity of the leadership, the corruption of the Government, the brutality of the police, the regime's indifference to the needs of the people for education, medical care, housing, for social justice and economic opportunity—all these, in Cuba as elsewhere, constituted an open invitation to revolution.[58]

Insurrection

Castro knew that preparations for the invasion he was planning were as incomplete as they had been for the Moncada misadventure, but Castro had learned that his organization had been infiltrated. He was forced to act before his enemies could fully prepare. On November 25, 1956, the armed men squeezed into the *Granma,* a weathered, creaking yacht. Their guns, ammunition, and food filled every available crevice.

The invasion had all the markings of a disaster. The fully laden yacht pitched and rolled through a Caribbean churning violently from autumn storms. A week later the Fidelistas disembarked, weak-kneed and hungry on the southeastern coast, where they found Batista's soldiers waiting. Of the eighty-two men who landed, only Castro, his brother Raul, Che Guevara, and thirteen others evaded the trap and made their way inland. The rest of his men were killed or captured by the Cuban army.

The lanky revolutionary led his men into the rugged high country of the Sierra Maestra. There, the revolutionaries, scrambling through thick brush and climbing into the mountains, eluded government forces. But was this really the force that would liberate Cuba from the tyranny of Batista? Castro tried to put the best face on the failure. Swaggering through the countryside, he is said to

After their failed 26th of July invasion, Castro's revolutionary soldiers retreated to the mountains of Cuba to regroup for their next assault.

have greeted the first peasant that he met with these words: "I am Fidel Castro and we have come to liberate Cuba."[59]

Castro's mad determination infected not only his comrades but also many of the Cubans that they encountered. News of Castro's return to the island drew supporters from around the country. Brigades were organized in remote outposts. Propaganda sheets were printed. And the romantic image of Fidel Castro, hero of the attack on Moncada, wading ashore with a handful of men to "liberate" Cuba caught the imagination of the people.

The revolution in some ways was a part of Castro. "The personality of the man is overpowering," recorded Herbert Matthews, a journalist who visited Cuba during the revolution. "It was easy to see that his men adored him and also to see why he has caught the imagination of the youth of Cuba all over the island. Here was an educated, dedicated fanatic, a man of ideals, of courage and of remarkable qualities of leadership."[60]

Constantly on the move, Castro and his men used a combination of sabotage, small firefights, and propaganda to wear down the thirty thousand professional soldiers of the Cuban army. As Batista's forces patrolled the island searching for the rebels, they were picked off in hit-and-run operations that struck fear into the army. Batista had already alienated much of the peasantry of Cuba through heavy taxation and cavalier treatment, and the soldiers were largely recruited from the lower classes, many of whom sympathized with Castro's rebellion. In the cities the workers went on general strike, and the government ground to a halt. The Cuban people had at last responded to Castro's dream of a popular uprising. Batista fled the country on January 1, 1959.

Havana, under Batista, had become a haven for the wealthy and for profiteers of all kinds—international gamblers, mafia bosses on the run from the authorities in the United States, and rich plantation owners. When Castro marched into the capital wearing his tattered green army fatigues, he promised an end to government corruption and the domination of the economy by foreign investors.

Historian Sebastian Balfour argues that Castro's success came from the long-suffering of the Cuban people at the hands of dictators and foreign occupation:

> The popularity of Castro can be attributed to a great extent to the fact that he came to symbolize for many Cubans a long-cherished hope of national liberation and social justice. When a dove alighted on his shoulder as he

Castro assumed control of Cuba in 1959, promising to restore democracy in the nation and end government corruption.

made his victory speech in Havana in 1959 the illusion was complete; it must have seemed to many there that Castro was predestined to realize the long-frustrated aspirations of almost a hundred years of struggle.[61]

At Odds with the "Yankee Imperialists"

Castro came to power as an unknown commodity to most of his countrymen: The majority of Cubans knew him only as a symbol of national pride and plucky opposition to tyranny. Few expected the hard-line Communism that Castro would establish in Cuba over the next decade.

Castro had vowed to restore the 1940 constitution, reinstating political freedoms in Cuba and making modest changes in the Cuban economy. He did nothing of the sort, however. Instead, he executed scores of Batista supporters to prevent them from opposing the new government and to take revenge for the hardships his men had suffered during the revolution. He also alienated rich landowners by instituting land reforms that threatened the traditional plantation economy.

As it became clearer that Castro was swept away by his own reformist zeal, many rich Cubans fled the country, taking their wealth and whatever expertise they possessed with them. Many of the Cubans who fled ended up in the United States, where government officials and business leaders watched Castro nervously.

U.S. fears of the nationalization of American-owned businesses were confirmed when Castro transferred ownership of these companies to the Cuban government. Diplomacy and trade moved hand in hand in the bitter exchanges between Washington, D.C., and Havana. For example, when American-owned oil refineries refused to process a shipment from the Soviet Union, Castro nationalized the refineries. The United States responded by eliminating laws that helped support the sugar industry, which was the basis for the Cuban economy. Of course, many Cuban sugarcane plantations were owned by American companies, so Castro, in turn, nationalized them.

Castro set out to redress some of the social injustice in Cuba. He instituted sweeping educational reforms that, over the next decade, sharply increased the literacy rate. Castro also fought against color prejudice in Cuba, which favored the light-skinned descendants of Spanish settlers over the darker-skinned descendants of the slaves that the Spanish brought to work the fields. Many of these goals were seen as constructive by some in the United States, but they received little praise because of Castro's belief in Communism and his unwillingness to allow political opponents to voice their opinions.

Confrontation with the United States escalated at a startling pace. In 1961 the United States broke off diplomatic relations with Cuba and secretly equipped thousands of Cuban exiles in the United States for an invasion designed to topple Castro. The president of the United States, John F. Kennedy, was determined not to allow a Communist state, the first in the Western Hemisphere, to thrive only ninety miles off the coast of Florida.

U.S. president John F. Kennedy, fearing the advance of Communism, planned an invasion of Cuba in 1961 to overthrow Castro.

Invaders at the Bay of Pigs

In April 1961 a group of hundreds of Cuban exiles, trained and equipped by the Central Intelligence Agency and the U.S. military, set sail for Cuba from Nicaragua. The U.S. Navy escorted them, and American planes flown by Cuban pilots bombed targets in Cuba in preparation for the invasion force to land on the coast.

One of the main objectives of the Cuban pilots flying American bombers was to destroy the Cuban air force so that it could not attack the invaders. That effort largely failed, and when the invasion force landed in the swampy region of the Bay of Pigs, they drew heavy fire from the Cuban army and were attacked from the air as well. American ships waiting offshore refused to use their firepower to support the invasion force and finally sailed away, leaving the invaders to be rounded up by Cuban troops.

The Bay of Pigs incident was a humiliating defeat for President Kennedy. The incident became a tremendous source of pride for Castro. After all, he had landed on Cuba with a poorly equipped force that was much smaller than the American-backed invasion force and had succeeded in conquering the island. From Castro's point of view, he had dealt a humiliating defeat to the world's greatest superpower.

One result of the Bay of Pigs invasion was the radicalization of the Castro regime. Faced with what he saw as an implacable foe, Castro tightened his control on the government and elevated the Communist Party to the exclusion of all opposition. Schools were transformed into ideological indoctrination centers, and all sectors of the economy soon fell under the government's control.

Hostile relations with the United States and economic isolation combined to push Castro into a close alliance with the Soviet Union. The Soviets delighted in their new ally and pumped millions of dollars of aid into Cuba. For the Soviet Union, locked in a struggle to spread Communism around the globe while the Americans attempted to head them off at every turn, Cuba was a godsend.

A Precious Soviet Ally

With the Soviet aid, Castro turned Cuba into an armed fortress. He imported tanks, munitions, and fighter jets from the Soviet Union, and he conscripted a large standing army. The island, which the United States had for so long intervened in at will, became a heavily armed Soviet outpost.

Cuba's status as a client of the Soviet Union also thrust the island into the middle of the Soviet-American relations, which were

Castro (left) formed an alliance with Soviet premier Nikita Khrushchev (right), who backed Communist Cuba financially and militarily.

becoming increasingly strained. Nikita Khrushchev, the Soviet premier, attempted to raise the stakes in 1962 by installing missiles armed with nuclear warheads on Cuba. The missiles were to be aimed at American cities, and their proximity to the United States would mean that American forces would have little time to respond should the order be given for their launch.

A tense period passed as President Kennedy threatened war if the Soviets did not remove their missiles. He sent the U.S. fleet to blockade the island from further Soviet missile shipments. The situation came to a head when the Soviets attempted to land twenty more warheads on the island.

In the end, without consulting Castro, Khrushchev withdrew the missiles. Castro was furious that the Russians had backed down, but the entire incident raised Castro's profile in international affairs. Castro's inclusion in the Soviet bloc made him a feared adversary of the United States.

Leftist Folk Hero

Throughout the Western Hemisphere, people witnessed on television the swaggering Cuban dictator delivering the long, fiery

In recent years, Castro has attempted to improve the failing Cuban economy by encouraging tourism and foreign investment.

speeches for which he was famous. His unkempt beard and green army fatigues became symbols of a new Communist order that some Latin Americans hoped would gel into a cohesive threat to American dominance in the Western Hemisphere.

Although Castro's attempts to foment revolution elsewhere in Latin America came to little, the Cuban leader saw to it that his nation continued to play a role in the world's affairs. For example, Cuban troops fought from 1975 to 1989 in Angola, where Communist rebels were fighting against forces backed by the United States.

Castro's willingness to send troops into combat in support of revolutions elsewhere was rewarded by the Soviet Union by increasing financial assistance to the struggling Cuban economy. Castro's social reforms had improved the lives of many of the Cuban people, but his nationalization of foreign companies and collectivization of agriculture had largely ruined Cuba's economy. As a result, Cuba became more and more dependent on Soviet aid.

This dependence on the USSR proved disastrous for Cuba when the Soviet Union began to break up in the early 1990s. Satellite countries in Eastern Europe began to break free of the Soviet Union but Castro remained a staunch supporter and a hungry recipient of Soviet aid.

Hard-Line Dictator; Crumbling Nation

In 1991 the Soviet Union began to unravel completely, and with it the Soviet economy. Pressed to provide for its own people, the Russian government could no longer support Cuba. The Cuban dictator had little choice but to loosen the government's control of the economy. Foreign investments returned in the form of joint ventures, and limited free enterprise was permitted. As a result, small businesses once again operate in the nation; however, since people are desperately poor, there is little money to spend in the privately owned shops that now exist.

In recent years Castro has wooed tourists to boost the Cuban economy. But the money that has been generated by tourism has made only party officials and a select few richer. The original promises of Castro's revolution have yet to be fulfilled.

Castro has repeatedly stated that he is willing to reopen relations with the United States, but Cuba has always been an irritant to the American government, and no accommodation has been found. In the 1990s, when Castro wooed business and tourism from Canada and Europe, the U.S. Congress reacted by tightening the economic blockade of Cuba.

The Cuban revolutionary who established a Communist state off the U.S. coast and repelled a U.S.-backed invasion has survived through the administrations of nine American presidents, from Eisenhower to Clinton. And it appears that no president is willing to make any concession with one of the world's last Communist hard-line dictators. What the future holds is uncertain, but Castro's talent for survival has earned him a lasting place in the roster of modern dictators.

CHAPTER 7

Saddam Hussein

In the predawn hours of August 2, 1990, the rumble of Soviet-made T-72 tanks sent guards along the Kuwait-Iraq border scrambling in confusion. As the tanks raced past the remote customs posts on the border, the guards could only assume that Saddam Hussein, the Iraqi strongman, had decided to enforce Iraq's historical claim to the tiny Persian Gulf emirate of Kuwait. On the heels of the tanks rumbled troop carriers and mobile artillery pieces, and helicopters broke the silence of the desert night with the rhythmic thudding of their rotor blades. The Iraqi invasion force dashed southward toward Kuwait City, sixty miles away.

When the invasion force reached Kuwait City, the capital, it encountered little resistance. The emir, the leader of Kuwait, fled to Saudi Arabia while his British-trained guards exchanged gunfire with the Iraqis, who quickly overwhelmed them. Before sunset on August 2, Iraq was in complete control of Kuwait.

In the Iraqi capital of Baghdad, Saddam Hussein proclaimed victory and fired his sidearm into the air in celebration. Guns were the favorite playthings of the Iraqi leader's youth, and they were never out of reach. His entire life had been a violent struggle. Snatching up his tiny neighbor and winning the praise of his people and the riches of Kuwait was no real challenge for the man the Americans were now calling "the Butcher of Baghdad."

Life in Tikrit

Saddam Hussein was born on April 28, 1937, in the village of al-Auja on the bank of the Tigris River. The nearest town of any size was Tikrit, once famous for its craftsmen who built rafts used to transport goods down the Tigris to Baghdad, about a hundred miles to the south. Though it lay on a major railway line, Tikrit and the surrounding villages were a backwater. Villagers lived in huts constructed of mud and reeds taken from the Tigris and used cow dung to fuel their cooking fires.

Saddam grew up in one of these tiny huts, with no electricity and no running water. It was a spartan existence, made worse by the cruelty of his stepfather. His real father, Hussein al-Majid, disappeared around the time Saddam was born. Official Iraqi biographies of Hussein claim that his father was killed by bandits, but this has never been independently confirmed; he may simply have abandoned the family. With his father absent, Hussein was given the name Saddam by his mother, which means "the one who confronts" or "the one who clashes."

Soon after Saddam was born, his mother, Subha, married Ibrahim Hassan, who gave the boy the chance to live up to his name. Hassan had little interest in another man's child, and he nagged Saddam constantly. "Get up you son of a whore," Hassan would say, "and look after the sheep."[62] Beatings sometimes accompanied his stepfather's harsh words, and young Hussein, in turn, became churlish and violent, frequently fighting with other village boys. His stepfather, who was illiterate, attempted to stop Saddam from going to school, but at the age of ten Saddam moved in with his uncle in Tikrit and enrolled in the local school.

At school, Saddam did not distinguish himself academically, but he did learn about his country's history. The British, who had

The Middle East

occupied Iraq through much of the nineteenth and into the twentieth century, were gone, but the monarchy the British had imposed on the country remained.

The British installed a prince from Saudi Arabia on the Iraqi throne. The Iraqi people never quite accepted the king, King Faisal I, or his descendants, whom they saw as foreigners. Iraq, carved from the remains of the Ottoman Empire after World War I, was still a tribal country in which people owed allegiance not to a nation or monarch but to fellow members of their family, their region, and their tribe.

Saddam's uncle had served in the Iraqi military, although he had been dismissed during World War II for joining a political party that was sympathetic to Germany and the Nazis. Nevertheless, Saddam loved to look at pictures of his uncle in uniform.

Saddam saw that military service offered an escape from village life, and he applied to the prestigious Baghdad Military Academy. But because of his low marks in school, he was rejected. Instead, he entered the Karch secondary

King Faisal I, a member of the Hashemite royal family, was installed on the Iraqi throne by the British.

school in Baghdad. It was at Karch that Saddam became interested in the Ba'ath nationalist movement.

Ba'athist Assassin

The Ba'ath movement was modeled after German and Italian Fascism. Its members emulated the fierce nationalism of Germany's Nazi Party and advocated military overthrow of the Iraqi monarch. Ba'ath members believed that all Arabs should cooperate in overthrowing the last remnants of colonial rule in the Middle East.

Through fellow Tikritis, Hussein quickly found a place among Ba'ath conspirators who were planning the king's overthrow. His willingness to use violence and enthusiasm for the cause made him valuable to the Ba'ath movement.

The Ba'athists were not the only opponents to the monarchy, however. In 1958 General Abdul Karim Kassem, although not a Ba'athist, overthrew the government of King Faisal II, a descendant of King Faisal I, ending the monarchy and instituting an Iraqi republic. Kassem was generally liked by much of the Iraqi populace, but the Ba'athists hated him for working with Iraq's Communist Party.

The Ba'ath movement turned to twenty-year-old Hussein to join a six-man hit team to assassinate Kassem. Hussein and his fellow assassins sprang into action, riddling Kassem's car with machine gunfire. But Kassem was well protected, and the assassination attempt failed. During the attack, a bullet struck Hussein in the leg. He later claimed that he ordered his comrades to dig out the bullet with a razor blade, after which he disguised himself as a Bedouin tribesman and escaped to Syria. A more likely story is that he was patched up in a Ba'ath safe house by a doctor who was sympathetic to the Ba'ath cause.

General Abdul Karim Kassem overthrew the monarchy and established a republic in Iraq in 1958. Soon after, he survived an assassination attempt by the Ba'athists.

Life in Exile

Hussein has been accused of exaggerating his role in the coup attempt, but his escape to Syria and then to Egypt is well documented. Once in Egypt, he was treated well since Egypt's leader, Gamal Abdel Nasser, shared Hussein's hatred for the Communist-backed Kassem. For the next four years, Saddam Hussein lived as a guest of the Egyptian government in an apartment in Cairo on the banks of the Nile River.

Hussein's living quarters were situated near Cairo University in a quarter called Dukkie. There, he associated with student radicals and other Ba'ath Party members while attending law classes at the university. Hussein was getting a first-rate education in Arab nationalism. A picture of him at this time shows the young Hussein donning a kaffiyeh, an Arab headdress, and wearing a thin mustache, a mark of manhood among many Arabs.

Hussein also married the daughter of his mentor, his Uncle Khayrallah, who sent his daughter, Sajidah, to Cairo for the ceremony. It was not unusual that he married his cousin, as many Iraqis have long done. Besides, by marrying a Tikriti and the daughter of his like-minded Ba'athist uncle, Hussein believed that he was surrounding himself with people he could trust. Hussein would always rely on fellow Tikritis and family members to help ensure the loyalty of those around him. Over the next years, Sajidah gave birth to several children, and Hussein's sons became the most trusted of all his inner circle.

In Cairo, Hussein closely followed news from Iraq. And in 1963 the Ba'athists struck again at Kassem; this time they succeeded in assassinating him. To rid Iraq of many of Kassem's most loyal followers, the Ba'athists unleashed a ferocious campaign of terror against his supporters and against other enemies of the Ba'ath Party. As a grisly threat of what could happen to enemies of the Ba'ath movement, General Kassem's bullet-riddled body was displayed on television. "The body was propped up on a chair in the studio," writes Samir al-Khalil, an Iraqi who fled after the Ba'athists took power. "A soldier sauntered around, handling its parts. . . . The whole macabre sequence closes with a scene that must forever remain etched on the memory of all those who saw it: the soldier grabbed the lolling head by the hair, came right up close, and spat full face into it."[63]

Rewarded for Violence

While the Ba'ath leaders set out to form a new government, Ba'ath soldiers seized the old royal palace, the Qasr-al-Nihayyah, or

"Palace of the End," where the royal family had once lived in splendor. This palace was converted into a torture chamber used to extract information from dissidents or punish them for their opposition. Hussein, now twenty-six, returned to Iraq to carve out a place for himself in the new government. He found his first job in the former palace interrogating suspects, extracting information through the use of rubber hoses and live electric wires.

The Ba'ath government ruled with violence and the threat of violence, and Hussein built up the Jihaz Haneen, the Ba'ath Party's internal security service, to carry out much of the violence. Members of the Jihaz Haneen regularly beat and killed opposition members. Eventually those who opposed the government were silenced with fear. Through his work with the Jihaz Haneen, Hussein won praise from the Ba'ath leaders and became feared even among their own ranks. His rapid rise to power was propelled primarily because other Ba'athists witnessed his deadly treatment of Ba'ath enemies and feared that he would do the same to them if they opposed him.

Family connections also aided Hussein's advancement. After his older cousin General Ahmad Hassan al-Bakr became secretary general of the party, Saddam was raised from torturer to deputy secretary general of the Ba'ath. In 1968 al-Bakr became Iraq's president and commander of the military. With Saddam Hussein at his side, al-Bakr once again set out to terrorize opposition with street violence, assassination, and ghoulish torture. Opposition was outlawed, and dissidents were arrested or murdered. Iraq became a one-party state.

In 1972 Iraq also nationalized the oil industry, which had been largely owned and operated by foreigners. Now Iraq's vast oil fields could be mined for the benefit solely of Iraq. Much of the money from the sale of oil, however, was pocketed by Ba'ath Party officials, so that the average Iraqi saw little improvement in his or her daily life. The new government gained some

General Ahmad Hassan al-Bakr, Hussein's cousin, became Iraq's president in 1968.

support from the Iraqi population, though, by redistributing land from the rich to the poor.

In addition to sharing the proceeds from the sale of oil, Hussein, al-Bakr's right-hand man, increased his own fortune and the fortune of his family by controlling Iraqi businesses. By enriching his family and organizing a vast network of secret police and spies, Hussein became the most powerful and most feared man in Iraq. Even al-Bakr feared Hussein's power, and for good reason.

The Feared Leader

In essence, Hussein and his relatives had turned Iraq into a family business. And as with many family businesses, advancement was impossible for Hussein while his relatives occupied senior jobs. In 1979 Hussein convinced al-Bakr—through hints of violence—to step aside. That July, al-Bakr resigned officially for health reasons, and Saddam Hussein became president of Iraq and chairman of the Revolutionary Command Council, the seat of real power in the Iraqi government.

To remove his last opponents in the Ba'ath Party, Hussein arranged for a spectacle of violence just after he took office. He gathered nearly a thousand senior Ba'ath Party members whom he distrusted in a closed meeting. In a large side room, Hussein made party members read statements, written for them, that proclaimed their guilt in conspiracies against Iraq and the Ba'ath Party. After the confessions were read, Hussein, with crocodile tears welling up in his eyes, condemned them to death. The entire spectacle was videotaped and distributed to Ba'ath Party members as a warning against further opposition.

Having consolidated his power within the Ba'ath Party, Hussein then set his propaganda machine to work convincing the Iraqi people that their new leader should be loved, even worshiped. Official biographers wrote colorful and fanciful accounts of his heroism during the days of the assassination attempt on Kassem and Hussein's escape from Iraq. State-controlled television and radio ran constant programs praising their new leader. And all over Baghdad squads of painters created murals of Hussein in heroic poses.

An Arab Martyr and His Ruinous War

The new Iraqi strongman professed to be not only the savior of his country but also the face of Arab nationalism. "The glory of the Arabs stems from the glory of Iraq," Hussein said. "Throughout history, whenever Iraq became mighty and flourished, so did the

Hussein flooded Iraq with propaganda, including huge murals of himself, embellished biographies, and television shows that sang his praises.

Arab Nation. This is why we are striving to make Iraq mighty, formidable, able and developed, and why we shall spare nothing to improve the welfare and to brighten the glory of the Iraqis."[64]

To prove his leadership in the Arab world, Hussein launched a military campaign against his neighbor, the non-Arab country of Iran, in 1980. Iran had undergone an Islamic revolution in 1979 that toppled the pro-Western government of the shah, or king, of Iran. Complicating an already unstable situation was the fact that Iran's new leaders were members of the Shiite sect of Islam while Iraq's leaders and a minority of its citizens were members of the Sunni sect. Hussein, convinced that Iran's Shiites hoped to topple his own government, ruthlessly suppressed the Shiite population in his own country. To counter what he saw as an external threat to his rule, he turned the full force of the Iraqi war machine against Iran.

As the war drained Iraq's financial resources, other Arab countries, along with the United States, rushed to Iraq's aid. Even with foreign arms shipments and heavy financial support from Arab countries, especially Kuwait and Saudi Arabia, Iraq's invasion of Iran was soon bogged down. Hussein directed the war personally, and frequently his strategy was ineffective. For example, Iraq's airpower was superior to Iran's, yet Hussein was reluctant to use it for fear of losing planes and pilots. Fortunately for Hussein, Iran's leadership was similarly inept militarily. The result was a long and bloody ground war. "The absence of military strategy," writes Iraqi dissident Samir al-Khalil, "when shared by both sides leads to grueling slogging matches in which nothing is more expendable than human life."[65]

In lieu of an effective military strategy, Hussein attempted to win victory by whipping Iraqi soldiers into a nationalist fervor. "Truly, you are the sword of God on Earth," he said, "and the heads you chop off are those of aggressive . . . backers of [Iran's Ayatollah] Khomeini, the maniac."[66]

For eight years, Hussein pursued his goal of destroy-ing his Iranian enemy. It was the most destructive, deadly war in modern Middle Eastern history. As al-Khalil comments, "Conducting a destructive war of this degree of reckless-ness takes two kinds of madness: to start it and to keep it going."[67]

Ayatollah Khomeini, who replaced the shah as leader of Iran in 1979, was seen by Hussein as a threat to his leadership in Iraq.

Down but Not Out

By 1988 the war had ground to a halt, and the Iranians signed a peace treaty with Iraq. Iraq, for all its suffering and financial ruin, had gained a strip of land along the Shatt al-Arab waterway, which runs between Kuwait and Iran and provides Iraq access to the Persian Gulf.

A Kurdish refugee caravan. The Kurds rebelled against Hussein, who responded by destroying their villages and killing many civilians.

The war bankrupted what had been an oil-rich nation. Iraq's economy was ruined, and inflation ran wild. Average citizens could barely afford common products as the Iraqi currency, the dinar, collapsed. For example, a roll of film cost the equivalent of about twenty-one dollars, a man's shirt cost about ninety dollars, a bottle of shampoo cost about twelve dollars.

Adding to the difficulties in Iraq, another group, the Kurds, had aspirations for a nation of their own and posed a constant threat to Hussein's control over the northern part of the country. Toward the end of the Iran-Iraq War, the Kurds rose against Hussein's regime. Hussein responded by sending elite units of his army, the Republican Guards, to put down the rebellion. The troops smashed entire villages, and on Hussein's orders, the Republican Guards shelled Kurdish villages with poison gas, killing many civilians. The brutal attack was the first documented instance of a government using poison gas on its own people.

To bolster the ruined Iraqi economy, Hussein turned once again to fellow Arab countries. In his pleas, Hussein argued that Iraq was entitled to financial help since it had defended the Arab world against the growing power of Iran. Arab leaders released some funds to Iraq, but they also reminded Hussein that Iraq already owed huge sums that had been borrowed during the Iran-Iraq War. Hussein was furious when his delegations came back from neighboring countries empty-handed. Kuwait in particular irritated the Iraqi dictator because, in his view, the oil-rich nation was overproducing oil and thus driving down the price that every oil-producing nation, including Iraq, got for its main export.

As Hussein seethed in Baghdad, his resentment toward his Arab neighbors grew. Finally, Hussein started massing troops along the border with Kuwait, first thirty thousand and eventually up to one hundred thousand men. The Kuwaitis, though alarmed, thought that Hussein was just trying to bully them into releasing more financial support.

The U.S. Central Intelligence Agency (CIA) took the threat more seriously, warning Washington of the possible invasion of Kuwait. April Glaspie, the American ambassador in Iraq, met with Hussein. At that meeting Glaspie inadvertently conveyed the impression that the United States would not defend Kuwait if Iraq invaded. "We have no opinion," Glaspie told Hussein, "on the Arab-Arab conflicts, like your border disagreement with Kuwait."[68]

Naked Aggression

On August 2, 1990, Iraqi forces seized the Gulf Emirate of Kuwait. The attack caught not only the Kuwaitis off guard but the international community as well. (Even in the United States, where the CIA had warned of the possibility of Iraq invading Kuwait, policymakers did not expect the prompt invasion.) Suddenly Western countries awakened to the danger that Hussein could squeeze off the supply of oil on which many of the world's economies depend.

Hussein had gambled that the Arab states and the international community would not go to war over Kuwait. He declared the Gulf state to be the nineteenth province of Iraq and pillaged the country of its wealth. Udai, Hussein's eldest son, organized the looting of cash, gold, and cars from Kuwait. In fact, Udai stole so many Kuwaiti luxury cars that his plundering of Kuwait could be characterized as the largest car heist in history.

Hussein, it turned out, had gambled unwisely. In an intense flurry of diplomatic activity, the world's leaders assembled the largest military coalition since World War II. The coalition arrayed against Hussein's forces included almost all of Iraq's Arab neighbors. The Arab leaders had decided that Hussein was just too dangerous to their own regimes, and they joined almost unanimously to drive him out of Kuwait.

The Persian Gulf War that ensued lasted just forty-three days, but more than one hundred thousand Iraqi soldiers perished in the conflict. Entrenched in positions along the Kuwaiti border, Iraq's army units were struck by massive bombing raids. Iraq's elite Republican Guards were decimated. During the one hundred hours of the allied ground assault, another sixty thousand Iraqi soldiers surrendered. Hussein's remaining forces beat a hasty retreat from Kuwait, and it seemed that Hussein's reign of terror was finally at an end.

But just as the allied forces neared Baghdad, military commanders received the order to stop their advance. The United Nations (UN) mandate, under which the United States and its allies were operating, only covered the expulsion of Iraqi troops from Kuwait, not the overthrow of Hussein. Seeing a way to remain in power, Hussein signed an unconditional surrender.

In Baghdad, Hussein heralded the end of the war as a victory. According to the Iraqi leader's version of events, he had fought off a coalition of the world's most powerful countries, including the

In a taped broadcast, Hussein tells Iraqis that they achieved victory against the United States.

United States, and survived. He called the Persian Gulf War "the Mother of All Battles," and he stood proudly having survived it. The tyrant had slipped the noose.

Caged but Not Tamed

As part of the terms of surrender, Hussein was forced to give up his so-called weapons of mass destruction and submit to UN weapons inspections to prove that he was really doing so. Early inspections revealed advanced nuclear, biological, and chemical weapons facilities. To the embarrassment of the United States, Great Britain, Germany, and other European countries, it was discovered that they had given much of the technology to Iraq during the Iran-Iraq War.

UN inspectors destroyed the weapons they found but became convinced that Hussein had carefully hidden key components of these weapons. In an ongoing cat-and-mouse game, Hussein repeatedly denied inspectors access to sites that might still conceal weapons of mass destruction.

The United Nations tried numerous times to force Hussein to adhere to the agreements he made through severe trade restrictions. By preventing other countries from trading with Iraq, the UN further impoverished Iraq. The suffering of the Iraqis as a result of

UN inspectors in Iraq believed Hussein still harbored weapons of mass destruction, but Hussein refused to allow the inspectors access to sites where they believed the weapons were stored.

these restrictions haunts some Arabs from other countries, and some governments in the Middle East have withdrawn support for the sanctions. The United States still leads the efforts to contain Iraq. American warplanes still patrol the northern and southern portions of Iraq. But Hussein has proven that time is on his side. How much longer Saddam Hussein will continue to rule Iraq remains an open question. For the time being, the rest of the world can only wait and watch to see what the wily dictator will do next.

NOTES

Chapter 1: The Dictator in the Twentieth Century

1. Quoted in David Fromkin, *A Peace to End All Peace: The Fall of the Ottoman Empire and the Creation of the Modern Middle East*. New York: Avon Books, 1989, inscription.

2. Charles L. Mee Jr., *The End of Order: Versailles, 1919*. New York: E. P. Dutton, 1980, p. 268.

3. Karl Marx and Friedrich Engels, *Basic Writings of Politics and Philosophy*, ed. Lewis Feuer. New York: Anchor Books, 1959, p. 109.

4. George Orwell, *Homage to Catalonia*. Boston: Beacon, 1967, p. 6.

5. Hugh Trevor-Roper, *The Last Days of Hitler*. New York: Macmillan, 1947, pp. 236–37.

6. Quoted in Martin Gilbert, *A History of the Twentieth Century, Volume One: 1900–1933*. New York: William Morrow, 1997, flap.

Chapter 2: Francisco Franco

7. Quoted in Edouard de Blaye, *Franco and the Politics of Spain*, trans. Brian Pearce. New York: Penguin Books, 1976, p. 51.

8. Quoted in de Blaye, *Franco and the Politics of Spain*, p. 51.

9. Quoted in Alan Lloyd, *Franco*. New York: Doubleday, 1969, p. 37.

10. Quoted in Lloyd, *Franco*, p. 27.

11. Quoted in Lloyd, *Franco*, p. 28.

12. Quoted in de Blaye, *Franco and the Politics of Spain*, p. 70.

13. Quoted in de Blaye, *Franco and the Politics of Spain*, p. 23.

14. Quoted in de Blaye, *Franco and the Politics of Spain*, p. 23.

15. Quoted in Lloyd, *Franco*, p. 14.

16. Quoted in Lloyd, *Franco*, p. 108.

17. Quoted in de Blaye, *Franco and the Politics of Spain*, p. i.

18. Quoted in de Blaye, *Franco and the Politics of Spain*, p. 549.

19. Quoted in Lloyd, *Franco*, p. 238.

Chapter 3: Adolf Hitler

20. Quoted in William Shirer, *The Rise and Fall of the Third Reich: A History of Nazi Germany*. New York: Simon & Schuster, 1960, inscription.

21. Quoted in Shirer, *The Rise and Fall of the Third Reich*, p. 6.

22. Quoted in Robert G. L. Waite, *The Psychopathic God: Adolf Hitler.* New York: Basic Books, 1977, p. 187.

23. Quoted in Shirer, *The Rise and Fall of the Third Reich*, p. 57.

24. Winston Churchill, *Memoirs of the Second World War.* Boston: Houghton Mifflin, 1987, p. 24.

25. Quoted in Shirer, *The Rise and Fall of the Third Reich*, p. 78.

26. Konrad Heiden, introduction to *Mein Kampf*, by Adolf Hitler, trans. Ralph Manheim. Boston: Houghton Mifflin, 1971, p. xv.

27. Quoted in Shirer, *The Rise and Fall of the Third Reich*, p. 5.

28. Shirer, *The Rise and Fall of the Third Reich*, p. xii.

29. Trevor-Roper, *The Last Days of Hitler*, p. 235.

30. Trevor-Roper, *The Last Days of Hitler*, p. 236.

Chapter 4: Joseph Stalin

31. Quoted in Albert Marrin, *Stalin: Russia's Man of Steel.* New York: Viking Kestrel, 1988, pp. 18–19.

32. Quoted in Robert Conquest, *Stalin: Breaker of Nations.* New York: Viking, 1991, p. 22.

33. Quoted in Conquest, *Stalin*, p. 87.

34. Quoted in Conquest, *Stalin*, p. 96.

35. Quoted in Conquest, *Stalin*, p. 100.

36. Quoted in Conquest, *Stalin*, p. 109.

37. Gilbert, *A History of the Twentieth Century*, p. 802.

38. Quoted in Conquest, *Stalin*, p. 247.

39. Quoted in Marrin, *Stalin*, p. 184.

40. Quoted in C. L. Sulzberger, *The American Heritage Picture History of World War II.* New York: Random House, 1994, p. 553.

41. Churchill, *Memoirs of the Second World War*, p. 997.

Chapter 5: Mao Zedong

42. Peter Carter, *Mao.* London: Oxford University Press, 1976, p. 9.

43. Jonathan D. Spence and Annping Chin, *The Chinese Century: A Photographic History of the Last Hundred Years.* New York: Random House, 1996, p. 49.

44. Mao Zedong, *Quotations from Chairman Mao Tsetung.* Peking: Foreign Languages, 1972, p. 12.

45. Quoted in James E. Sheridan, *China in Disintegration: The Republican Era in Chinese History, 1912–1949.* New York: Free Press, 1975, p. 277.

46. Quoted in C. P. FitzGerald, *Mao Tse-Tung and China.* New York: Penguin Books, 1976, p. 68.

47. Quoted in John Bartlett, *Familiar Quotations: A Collection of Passages, Phrases, and Proverbs Traced to Their Sources in Ancient and Modern Literature.* 16th ed. Boston: Little, Brown, 1992, p. 436.

48. Quoted in Arthur Cotterell, *China: A Cultural History.* New York: Mentor, 1990, p. 290.

49. Mao, *Quotations from Chairman Mao Tsetung,* pp. 302–303.

50. Mao, *Quotations from Chairman Mao Tsetung,* p. 300.

51. Quoted in Cotterell, *China,* p. 295.

52. Quoted in Spence and Chin, *The Chinese Century,* p. 203.

53. Quoted in *Baedeker's China.* New York: Macmillan Travel, 1996, p. 75.

Chapter 6: Fidel Castro

54. Quoted in Herbert Matthews, *Fidel Castro.* New York: Simon & Schuster, 1969, p. 23.

55. Quoted in Sebastian Balfour, *Castro.* London: Longman, 1980, p. 31.

56. Quoted in Matthews, *Fidel Castro,* p. 24.

57. Quoted in Balfour, *Castro,* p. 37.

58. Quoted in Matthews, *Fidel Castro,* p. 51.

59. Quoted in Balfour, *Castro,* p. 48.

60. Matthews, *Fidel Castro,* p. 113.

61. Balfour, *Castro,* p. 3.

Chapter 7: Saddam Hussein

62. Quoted in Judith Miller and Laurie Mylroie, *Saddam Hussein and the Crisis in the Gulf.* New York: Times Books, 1990, p. 26.

63. Quoted in Miller and Mylroie, *Saddam Hussein and the Crisis in the Gulf,* p. 31.

64. Quoted in Miller and Mylroie, *Saddam Hussein and the Crisis in the Gulf,* p. 41.

65. Samir al-Khalil, *Republic of Fear: The Inside Story of Saddam's Iraq.* New York: Pantheon Books, 1989, p. 281.

66. Quoted in al-Khalil, *Republic of Fear,* p. 281.

67. al-Khalil, *Republic of Fear,* p. 282.

68. Quoted in Miller and Mylroie, *Saddam Hussein and the Crisis in the Gulf,* p. 18.

Chronology

1911
The last Chinese emperor is overthrown by Republican forces.

1914
World War I begins.

1915
Poison gas is first used by the Germans in warfare.

1917
Bolsheviks led by Lenin seize power in Russia, toppling the Russian monarchy.

1918
Russia withdraws from World War I; the German kaiser abdicates; World War I ends.

1919
The Treaty of Versailles officially ends World War I and causes economic devastation in Germany; League of Nations is founded; Benito Mussolini introduces Fascism in Italy.

1921
Mao Zedong helps found the Chinese Communist Party.

1922
Union of Soviet Socialist Republics is established; Mussolini is named prime minister of Italy.

1923
Adolf Hitler forms the National Socialist (Nazi) Party in Germany.

1924
Stalin succeeds Lenin as leader of the Soviet Union.

1927
Chiang Kai-shek's purge of the Communists from the Kuomintang leads to civil war.

1929
U.S. stock market crash triggers a worldwide depression.

1931
Japanese establish a puppet state in Manchuria; Spain becomes a republic; King Alfonso is deposed.

1933
Hitler becomes chancellor of Germany and purges opposition; Stalin purges opposition in Russia.

1934
Hitler assumes title of "führer," or leader of the German people; Mao starts the Long March.

1935

Hitler renounces the Versailles treaty and begins rebuilding the German army.

1936

Formation of the Axis, an alliance between Germany and Italy; Franco begins the Spanish Civil War.

1937

Japanese invade China, capturing Beijing and Shanghai; German aircraft bomb Spain in support of Franco.

1938

Germany annexes Austria and gains Czechoslovakia's Sudetenland in Munich Pact.

1939

Germany annexes Czechoslovakia; Franco captures Madrid; the Spanish Civil War ends; Germany invades Poland, triggering World War II.

1940

Germany invades France, Belgium, Denmark, and Norway; Japan joins the Berlin-Rome Axis.

1941

Germany invades Russia; Japanese bomb Pearl Harbor, causing the United States to declare war on the Axis powers.

1943

Germans surrender to Russians at Stalingrad.

1944

Allies invade Normandy, causing German forces to retreat.

1945

Germany surrenders; Hitler commits suicide; United States drops atomic bombs on the Japanese cities of Hiroshima and Nagasaki; Japan surrenders, ending World War II; Potsdam Conference discusses postwar settlements.

1946

League of Nations is replaced by United Nations; German war crimes trials are held in Nuremberg.

1947

Marshall Plan aids European war recovery.

1948

Nation of Israel is established, setting off war between Israel and the Arab League; Berlin is blockaded by the Soviet Union.

1949

Mao Zedong proclaims the People's Republic of China; Nationalists withdraw to the island of Taiwan; Germany is divided into East Germany and West Germany; North American Treaty Organization (NATO) is formed.

1950
North Korean troops invade South Korea.

1953
Stalin dies.

1956
Egypt nationalizes the Suez Canal.

1957
Fidel Castro begins revolution in Cuba.

1959
Castro overthrows Batista and becomes premier of Cuba.

1961
Bay of Pigs invasion of Cuba fails.

1962
Cuban Missile Crisis.

1966
Cultural Revolution begins in China.

1971
Communist China replaces Taiwan in United Nations.

1972
President Richard Nixon travels to China to renew relations.

1975
Franco dies.

1976
Mao dies.

1979
Ayatollah Khomeini gains control of Iran, ousting the shah; Iranians seize U.S. embassy in Tehran, beginning the hostage crisis; Saddam Hussein becomes president of Iraq.

1980
Iran-Iraq War begins.

1988
Iran-Iraq War ends.

1990
Iraq invades Kuwait.

1991
Allied coalition drives Iraq out of Kuwait in the Persian Gulf War.

1996
U.S. Helms-Burton Act tightens economic embargo on Cuba.

For Further Reading

Eleanor H. Ayer, *The Importance of Adolf Hitler.* San Diego: Lucent Books, 1996. In her short biography, Ayer places the mad reign of Hitler in the context of the twentieth century and also discusses the events of his life.

Judith Bently, *Fidel Castro of Cuba.* New York: Julian Messner, 1991. A good overview of the leader of the first Communist nation in the Western Hemisphere.

Don E. Beyer, *Castro.* New York: Franklin Watts, 1993. A detailed and thoughtful account of Castro's life and leadership.

Warren Brown, *Fidel Castro: Cuban Revolutionary.* Brookfield, CT: Millbrook, 1994. A short overview of Castro's life with particular attention to the insurrection that installed Castro as the head of the Cuban nation.

Janet Caulkins, *Joseph Stalin.* New York: Franklin Watts, 1990. A biography full of quotes and descriptions of the events in the life of one of the world's most brutal dictators.

Rebecca Stefoff, *Saddam Hussein.* Brookfield, CT: Millbrook, 1995. This excellent short biography gives a vivid picture of Hussein's childhood and covers his life through the Gulf War.

WORKS CONSULTED

Rick Atkinson, *Crusade: The Untold Story of the Persian Gulf War.* Boston: Houghton Mifflin, 1993. Atkinson gives a blow-by-blow account of the allied coalition's confrontation with Saddam Hussein's armies in Kuwait and Iraq.

Baedeker's China. New York: Macmillan Travel, 1996. This guide to travel in the People's Republic of China includes essays on the nation's topography, economy, history, arts, and culture.

Sebastian Balfour, *Castro.* London: Longman, 1980. A study of Castro in light of the Cuban Revolution and the historical forces that shaped his victory.

John Bartlett, *Familiar Quotations: A Collection of Passages, Phrases, and Proverbs Traced to Their Sources in Ancient and Modern Literature.* 16th ed. Boston: Little, Brown, 1992. This collection of familiar sayings also contains information on those who originated them.

Edouard de Blaye, *Franco and the Politics of Spain.* Trans. Brian Pearce. New York: Penguin Books, 1976. A rich, authoritative study of Franco's rise to power and the situation in Spain that fostered it. De Blaye's study is especially strong on political and economic analysis of Spain before and during Franco's rule.

Alan Bullock, *Hitler: A Study in Tyranny.* New York: Harper & Row, 1971. Perhaps the standard biography of Adolf Hitler, by British historian Alan Bullock.

James Bunting, *Adolf Hitler.* Folkstone, England: Bailey Brothers and Swinfen, 1973. An excellent synopsis of Hitler's struggle for and grip on power.

Peter Carter, *Mao.* London: Oxford University Press, 1976. A short, evocative summary of Mao Zedong's life.

Wilber A. Chaffee Jr. and Gary Prevost, eds., *Cuba: A Different America.* Totowa, NJ: Rowman & Littlefield, 1989. A collection of essays on social, economic, and political conditions and policies in Castro's Cuba.

Jerome Chen, *Mao and the Chinese Revolution.* London: Oxford University Press, 1965. A detailed, well-documented account of Mao's rise to power and the evolution of the victory of the Communist Party. Includes thirty-seven poems by Mao Zedong.

Winston Churchill, *Memoirs of the Second World War.* Boston: Houghton Mifflin, 1987. A firsthand account of World War II from the British prime minister who proved to be Hitler's most implacable foe.

Robert Conquest, *Stalin: Breaker of Nations.* New York: Viking, 1991. One of the first biographies by a Western scholar that draws on records opened during the collapse of the Soviet Union.

Arthur Cotterell, *China: A Cultural History.* New York: Mentor, 1990. A cultural history of China from the Bronze Age to the 1980s.

Adel Darwish and Gregory Alexander, *Unholy Babylon: The Secret History of Saddam's War.* New York: St. Martin's, 1991. Egyptian-born Middle East correspondent for the *Independent,* a British daily, and his coauthor Gregory Alexander give a detailed account of the West's support of Saddam Hussein and a portait of Iraq under his rule.

C. P. FitzGerald, *Mao Tse-Tung and China.* New York: Penguin Books, 1976. A concise introduction to the life of Mao Zedong, the Communist revolution in China, and the changing nature of China's Communist dictatorship.

Anne Fremantle, ed., *Mao Tse-tung: An Anthology of His Writings.* New York: Mentor Books, 1962. A collection of some of Mao's writings, divided into two sections: political and strategic writings and philosophical writings.

David Fromkin, *A Peace to End All Peace: The Fall of the Ottoman Empire and the Creation of the Modern Middle East.* New York: Avon Books, 1989. A lively account of the Middle East just before and after World War I and the colonial nations carved out of the Ottoman Empire by the colonial bureaus of France and Great Britain.

Martin Gilbert, *A History of the Twentieth Century, Volume One: 1900–1933.* New York: William Morrow, 1997. A year-by-year account of world history for the first thirty-four years of the twentieth century.

Jean Grugel and Tim Rees, *Franco's Spain.* New York: Arnold, 1997. A scholarly examination of politics and policies in Francoist Spain.

Maurice Halperin, *The Rise and Decline of Fidel Castro: An Essay in Contemporary History.* Berkeley and Los Angeles: University of California Press, 1972. A detailed and well-documented account of the Cuban Revolution and Castro's political policies.

Adolf Hitler, *Mein Kampf.* Trans. Ralph Manheim. Boston: Houghton Mifflin, 1971. The turgid autobiography of Hitler, in which he spells out his ghoulish plan for a Nazi state; written during his imprisonment in 1924–1925.

Ian Kershaw, *Hitler*. New York: Longman, 1991. A shorter work by a well-respected Hitler biographer and historian of Nazi Germany.

Samir al-Khalil, *Republic of Fear: The Inside Story of Saddam's Iraq*. New York: Pantheon Books, 1989. An Iraqi who fled Hussein's regime outlines the ruthless nature of Iraq under the Ba'athist dictator and his party.

Henry Kissinger, *Diplomacy*. New York: Simon & Schuster, 1994. A lucid study of European and American foreign relations and the diplomats who shaped them, written by President Nixon's secretary of state.

Alan Lloyd, *Franco*. New York: Doubleday, 1969. A swift narrative concentrating on Franco's rise to power and the Spanish Civil War.

Peter Mansfield, *The Arabs*. New York: Penguin Books, 1992. An overview of the rise of Arab nationalism, with chapters on the political situation in Middle Eastern states today.

Albert Marrin, *Stalin: Russia's Man of Steel*. New York: Viking Kestrel, 1988. A short, colorful biography of Stalin for young adult readers.

Helmut Martin, *Cult and Canon: The Origins and Development of State Maoism*. New York: M. E. Sharpe, 1982. A study of Mao's political writings and their role in the formation of the Chinese Communist state and the development of the cult of Mao.

Karl Marx and Friedrich Engels, *Basic Writings of Politics and Philosophy*. Ed. Lewis Feuer. New York: Anchor Books, 1959. A collection of works by two celebrated Communist thinkers, including the Communist Manifesto.

Herbert Matthews, *Fidel Castro*. New York: Simon & Schuster, 1969. A biography of the Cuban dictator by a *New York Times* correspondent who covered Castro's revolution. Rich in detail and anecdotes.

Charles L. Mee Jr., *The End of Order: Versailles, 1919*. New York: E. P. Dutton, 1980. A brilliant, entertaining account of the treaty negotiations that formally ended World War I.

Judith Miller and Laurie Mylroie, *Saddam Hussein and the Crisis in the Gulf*. New York: Times Books, 1990. Miller, a *New York Times* Middle East correspondent, and Mylroie, a Harvard University professor of Middle Eastern studies, published this primer just months after the Gulf War to explain the rise of Saddam Hussein and the origins of the conflict.

George Orwell, *Homage to Catalonia*. Boston: Beacon, 1967. A first-hand account of the famous novelist's time with the International Brigade during the Spanish Civil War.

Edvard Radzinsky, *Stalin: The First In-Depth Biography Based on Explosive New Documents from Russia's Secret Archives.* New York: Doubleday, 1996. A sensationalistic new biography by a Russian playwright and historian that draws heavily from sources disclosed after the collapse of the Soviet Union.

Eduardo del Rius, *Mao for Beginners.* New York: Pantheon Books, 1980. An entertaining and informative summary of Mao's life through text and illustrations by the left-leaning Mexican journalist Rius.

James E. Sheridan, *China in Disintegration: The Republican Era in Chinese History, 1912–1949.* New York: Free Press, 1975. A detailed account of China from the overthrow of the last emperor to the founding of the People's Republic of China.

William L. Shirer, *The Rise and Fall of the Third Reich: A History of Nazi Germany.* New York: Simon & Schuster, 1960. A firsthand account of Germany under Hitler by a CBS foreign correspondent.

Jean Edward Smith, *George Bush's War.* New York: Henry Holt, 1992. A look at President George Bush's role in launching the Gulf War. Full of interesting details about the American motives and relations with other allied governments.

Edgar Snow, *Red Star over China.* New York: Grove, 1961. The first book about the Chinese Communists, written by an American journalist who became sympathetic with Mao after spending time at the Yan'an base camp. The Grove edition of the book, originally published in 1938, is introduced by China scholar John Fairbank.

Jonathan D. Spence and Annping Chin, *The Chinese Century: A Photographic History of the Last Hundred Years.* New York: Random House, 1996. A study of China from the fall of the Qing dynasty to the Tiananmen Square incident in pictures and words.

C. L. Sulzberger, *The American Heritage Picture History of World War II.* New York: Random House, 1994. A well-written introduction to World War II through text and numerous black-and-white and color photographs.

H. R. Trevor-Roper, *The Last Days of Hitler.* New York: Macmillan, 1947. A study of the closing years of the Third Reich and the days leading up to Hitler's suicide. Trevor-Roper, who marched into Berlin with the British army in the final days of the war, believes that history is shaped by the personalities of great men as much as it is by social and economic forces.

Robert G. L. Waite, *The Psychopathic God: Adolf Hitler.* New York: Basic Books, 1977. A psychological study that attempts to plumb the depths of Hitler's mind using anecdotal evidence and psychoanalysis.

Zhong Wenxian, ed., *Mao Zedong: Biography, Assessment, Reminiscences*. Beijing: Foreign Languages, 1986. A fascinating look at Mao and Maoism in a collection of essays by Chinese and non-Chinese citizens and published by the state-supervised Foreign Languages Press on the tenth aniversary of the death of Mao Zedong.

Mao Zedong, *Quotations from Chairman Mao Tsetung*. Peking: Foreign Languages, 1972. A collection of revolutionary aphorisms collected in a pocket-size red book that fueled the Cultural Revolution.

INDEX

PICTURE CREDITS

ABOUT THE AUTHOR

Robert Green holds an M.A. in journalism from New York University and a B.A. in English literature from Boston University. He is the author of fourteen other books including *China* for Lucent Books and biographies of Alexander the Great, Tutankhamen, Julius Caesar, Hannibal, Herod the Great, and Cleopatra, as well as biographies of six British monarchs and *Viva La Franco: The French Resistance During World War II*. He lives in New York City.